ANGLES
ON THE ENGLISH-SPEAKING WORLD

VOLUME 5

Charting Shakespearean Waters:
Text and Theatre

Editors: Niels Bugge Hansen and Søs Haugaard

ANGLES
ON THE ENGLISH-SPEAKING WORLD

VOLUME 5

Charting Shakespearean Waters:
Text and Theatre

Editors: Niels Bugge Hansen
and Søs Haugaard

MUSEUM TUSCULANUM PRESS
UNIVERSITY OF COPENHAGEN
2005

Published for
The Department of English,
University of Copenhagen

*

EDITORIAL BOARD

DORTE ALBRECHTSEN   RUSSELL DUNCAN

LENE ØSTERMARK-JOHANSEN

BOOK REVIEW EDITOR
CHARLES LOCK

*

Angles on the English-Speaking World is published once a year by the Department of English at the University of Copenhagen. Issues are thematic and contain a balance of articles from local and international contributors. *Angles* is intended as a lively forum for a broad range of literary, linguistic, cultural and historical studies from various theoretical standpoints.

*

Articles for consideration and all editorial communication should be sent in three copies to:
Angles on the English-Speaking World
University of Copenhagen, Department of English
Njalsgade 130, DK-2300 Copenhagen S, Denmark

Business communications, including subscriptions and orders for reprints, should be addressed to the publishers:

MUSEUM TUSCULANUM PRESS
Njalsgade 94, DK-2300 Copenhagen S, Denmark
www.mtp.dk

*

Cover design by Henrik Maribo based on a hand-coloured engraving entitled *Monde dans une tête de fou* (ca. 1590). Bibliothèque nationale de France.

Set by Anna Henneberg and Pia Theilgaard Smith

Printed in Denmark by Kopi Service at the Faculty of Humanities, University of Copenhagen

© 2005 MUSEUM TUSCULANUM PRESS &
ANGLES ON THE ENGLISH-SPEAKING WORLD
New Series, volume 5

ISBN 87-635-0261-5
ISSN 0903-1723

CONTENTS

Editors' Preface 7

Introduction 8

Peter Holland
Coasting in the Mediterranean: The Journeyings of *Pericles* 11

Tom Pettitt
Midsummer Metadrama:
'Pyramus and Thisbe' and Early English Household Theatre 31

Dorrit Einersen
Shakespeare's *Troilus and Cressida*:
Tragedy, Comedy, Satire, History or Problem Play? 45

Michael Skovmand
Troilus and Cressida: A Dialogic Reading 57

Charles Lock
Soiling the Page, Daubing the Wall:
A Reading of *Henry the Fourth, Part One*, 1.1. 1-65 73

Søs Haugaard
'Now is he turned orthography': On Silence and Writing 85

Lars Kaaber
What Happened to *Hamlet*? Text and Tradition 97

Robert Weimann
Hamlet and the Players:
Performance and Appropriation of Shakespeare in East-Berlin 109

Paul Edmondson
Macbeth: The Play in Performance 121

Viggo Hjørnager Pedersen
As They Liked It:
Departures from Shakespeare's Text in Two Adaptations of
As You Like It: 135

Niels Bugge Hansen
The Spirit of Transformation:
Shakespeare's *The Tempest* and Karen Blixen's 'Tempests' 147

Book Review 159

Notes on Contributors.. 162

Forthcoming Issues 165

EDITORS' PREFACE

The editors of this volume of *Angles* are proud to be able to present this collection of essays on Shakespeare. As reflected in the title, CHARTING SHAKESPEAREAN WATERS: TEXT AND THEATRE, the volume contains a wide range of subjects on many different plays. We have not wished to impose any specific focus on the volume, but rather chosen our contributors and invited them to write articles that reflect their current interests in Shakespeare.

We are delighted that so many who were asked agreed readily to give us a paper, so that our initial intentions have been realized. We wanted the volume to demonstrate the lively interest in Shakespeare which flourishes within our own department (Bugge Hansen, Einersen, Haugaard, Hjørnager Pedersen, Lock). We also wanted the book to reflect the state of Shakespeare studies at our Danish sister universities and at the same time to strengthen the links to them (Pettitt, Skovmand). It is likewise a pleasure to include a representative of the many Danish Shakespeareans outside the universities who nourish the interest in our dramatist through writing and performance (Kaaber).

In addition we wanted to draw on international scholars who over a long period and in various capacities have become friends of the department. It is a great joy that we can count such distinguished Shakespeareans among our friends, and that they have been so ready to contribute and thus give our publication an international dimension. The hub in this network is Stratford-upon-Avon, home of the Shakespeare Institute and the Shakespeare Centre. Contacts made at the International Shakespeare Conferences resulted in Robert Weimann's lecturing at Copenhagen University many years ago and subsequent links with the German *Shakespeare Gesellschaft*. Peter Holland accepted an invitation to come to Copenhagen and lecture when he was Director of the Shakespeare Institute. Finally, we are very pleased to count Paul Edmondson, Educational Director at the Shakespeare Centre, among our contributors and friends, both for his own services as organizer and lecturer to Copenhagen groups, and as the current representative of an institution which for decades has welcomed Danish students and lovers of Shakespeare in pursuit of Stratford's unique academic and dramatic possibilities.

We thank them all and wish that our readers may find as much enjoyment in reading this collection of essays as we have had in editing it.

Niels Bugge Hansen
Søs Haugaard

INTRODUCTION

The essays in this volume have not been written to fit in with an over-all theme. They are here because they are about Shakespeare: Shakespeare as text and Shakespeare as theatre: Shakespeare in his age and Shakespeare through the ages. All the same, these eleven articles, besides showing many different ways of thinking and writing about Shakespeare, do fall into a pattern of a kind, if read together and in the order they are printed.

Peter Holland's article on *Pericles*, Shakespeare's 'play of the sea *par excellence*', sets the reader on a course of cruising, and not only with Pericles in the Mediterranean. The Elizabethan sailors' distinction between pilotage and navigation becomes an image of the way the old story of Apollonius has travelled from narrative to drama with Shakespeare as pilot, 'striking out in grand navigational gestures across unmapped territory to create the exhilarating immediacy of the here of drama, starting from the there of the old story.' Starting in the Mediterranean, we have embarked on a journey which will in the end take us to the seacoast of Norway.

Tom Pettitt moves the scene from the hazards of the sea to 'the poorly mapped territory on the borders between the stage, pageantry and seasonal custom'. The performance of the rude mechanicals in *A Midsummer Night's Dream* is shown to reflect a traditional pattern in community theatre performed at stately mansions in the early English period. The comedy not only depicts but also recreates the household revels in its own tripartite structure.

Dorrit Einersen maps the progress of the story of Troilus and Cressida from medieval writers to Shakespeare and discusses the vexed question of the genre of Shakespeare's version of the story. As it is neither genuinely tragic nor comic, she concludes, in the manner of Polonius, that it 'can perhaps be called a historical-tragical-comical-satirical-problem play'.

The question of genre is carried on in **Michael Skovmand's** paper on *Troilus and Cressida*. His dialogic reading of the play, based on its diegetic and mimetic dimensions, examines the counterpoint of opposing discourses within the scenes and between the scenes, but also includes a metadiegetic dimension. The organizing principles of 'actively competing voices and the renunciation of positive authorization' are particularly clearly in evidence in the counterpoint of voices in the love scene between Troilus and Cressida (III,2).

From the matter of Troy back to English soil. **Charles Lock's** paper starts with a discussion of the imprint of marks on pages and walls in the early modern period, which leads to a detailed explication of the opening lines of

Henry IV, Part One. It is in particular the origins, meanings and uses of the word 'soil' in this passage which are in focus, as in the line of the man (or horse) 'stained with the variation of each soil'. Just as there are imprints of soles on soil, so soil may leave tell-tale marks on other surfaces. As readers, we need to be alert to the inscription of marks on walls and surfaces other than pages.

Søs Haugaard's article is also about writing, and about the power of language to give life and identity to characters in Shakespeare's dramatic works. The interplay of language and silence in drama is used to analyse a recurrent theme in Shakespeare's sonnets, which are explored as a mode of drama between the voice of the poet and the 'soundless deep' of the young man.

The nautical imagery in sonnet 80 keeps alive this volume's idea of cruising and charting. At the same time this paper, in its concern with dramatic performance, forms a bridge to the remaining essays, which deal with the various ways the Shakespearean texts have survived on the stage, travelled and been appropriated to the present day.

Lars Kaaber traces the vicissitudes of *Hamlet*, as text and as theatre, from the 17th century to the present day. Following Shaw's wish to see *Hamlet* 'as Shakespeare meant it', Kaaber's survey ends with a plea for a return on the stage from the Romantic hero to the Hamlet described in Shakespeare's text: 'callous, self-centred, pesky and brutal.'

Robert Weimann uses Benno Besson's production of *Hamlet* in East Berlin in 1977, and in particular its rendering of the scene of Hamlet's advice to the players, to discuss the role of performance in relation to society: 'the appropriation of Shakespeare in East German post-war theatre and criticism constituted a public site on which cultural communications inhabited an ambivalent space between political control and unorthodoxy, between ideological dogma and a search for a forceful, irrepressible performative.'

Performance is also the subject matter of **Paul Edmondson's** paper. Working from the importance of the opening scene of *Macbeth* and the role of the witches he discusses how 'the dramatic crises arise out of, and develop through, several key moments … and how these might become manifest in a production.' He invites his readers to consider a series of choices which *en route* from the page to the stage face the director as interpreter of the text, and which each reader also needs to think about.

Viggo Hjørnager Pedersen's paper deals with the translation into Danish, or perhaps rather the adaptation, of *As You Like It*, done by Sille Beyer in the 19th century. Like George Sand's translation of the same comedy into French in the same period, Beyer's text avoids the bawdy, the carnal and the cynical facets in Shakespeare's comedy of love. This supports the view that translators 'tend to adapt their texts to the literary norms of their culture.'

Niels Bugge Hansen's essay rounds off the charting of Shakespearean themes, then and now. Karen Blixen appropriated *The Tempest* for a story set in 19th century Norway. In 'Tempests' a girl chosen to play Ariel identifies with her role in a real storm at sea and has to pay the price in human terms. In the process she becomes an image of the artist's predicament.

COASTING IN THE MEDITERRANEAN: THE JOURNEYINGS OF *PERICLES*

PETER HOLLAND

Poor Pericles! After his unfortunate visit to Antioch where he proves that it is not necessarily good to be as good a solver of riddles as Oedipus, his wise advisor Helicanus, 'Fit counselor and servant for a prince',[1] gives him the following advice:

> Well, my lord, since you have given me leave to speak,
> Freely will I speak....
> Therefore my lord, go travel for a while,... (1.2.100-1, 104)

And, though Helicanus puts a period on this travel-time, an end to the cruising in the Med which is Pericles' best course of safety ('Till that his rage and anger be forgot, / Or till the destinies do cut his thread of life' [105-6]), Pericles hardly stops travelling in the action of the play thereafter.

My wish to offer this consideration of *Pericles* to this collection is in part prompted by the memory of taking the train across the bridge from Denmark to Sweden, of experiencing how a sea-journey had become a road and rail one, of seeing a link between nations transformed and a stretch of water that could only have been travelled in one way suddenly and magnificently altering. But my specific interest in this, in the threat to Pericles of limitless cruising, was driven by a moment in the play and the accompanying note in the fascinating DelVecchio/Hammond edition of *Pericles*. In the middle of the play's second storm, in act 3, with the birth of Marina and the apparent death in childbirth of Thaisa, as Pericles is forced to accept the sailors' superstition and have Thaisa's corpse thrown overboard, buried at sea, he turns to one of the sailors:

>   Mariner, say, what coast is this?
> *Master.*   We are near Tarsus.
> *Pericles.*   Thither, gentle mariner,
>   Alter thy course for Tyre. When canst thou reach it?
> *Master.*   By break of day, if the wind cease.
> *Pericles.*   O, make for Tarsus! (3.1.72-5)

As DelVecchio and Hammond note here, 'If Pentapolis is in Greece, as the play declares, a glance at the map…would suggest that any reasonable course from thence to Tyre would not go anywhere near Tarsus' (*ad loc.*, p.138). And if you check the map of the Eastern Mediterranean which always accompanies editions of *Pericles*,[2] you will see that they are right. Surely you would go straight across the middle, passing on the south side of Cyprus, as the shortest distance between Greece and Tyre.

In the last few years maps have become a subject of great importance in early modern studies.[3] Little of this work has looked specifically at *Pericles*[4] but this is a play peculiarly defined by maps and by sailing. *Pericles* is a remarkable play not least in its choice of locations: every single scene takes place either at sea or in a town or other place that is a port or is on the seacoast. It is not only that the play's action crisscrosses the Mediterranean but also that its view of that movement is entirely driven by the perception of the sea as the crucial linking feature. It is the play of the sea *par excellence*, a play controlled by the sustained awareness of the sea as apparently the only means of journeying from one place to another, whatever other symbolic significances the expanse of water may have and however that might connect with Shakespeare's continual interest in those symbolic potentials throughout his career. No-one seems to make an overland journey (though it is just possible that the king's city of Pentapolis is inland from the seacoast where Pericles washes up after the first storm). The sea is the web that links and binds, drawing lines on the map, following the roads and routes in the sea that preserves no trace of them.

DelVecchio and Hammond begin their comments with the phrase 'If Pentapolis is in Greece'. It certainly seems to be at first hearing. When Pericles turns up on that particular seacoast after the ship and the whole of the ship's company has gone down at sea, he entreats the fishermen for pity, 'He asks of you that never used to beg' (2.1.61). The First Fisherman's reply places the scene firmly and unequivocally: 'No, friend, cannot you beg? Here's them in our country of Greece gets more with begging than we can do with working' (2.1.62-4). It is not till later in the scene that the name of this part of the country of Greece is spoken:

1 *Fisherman*.	Hark you, sir, do you know where ye are?
Pericles.	Not well.
1 *Fisherman*.	Why, I'll tell you. This is called Pentapolis and our king, the good Simonides. (2.1.93-6)

King Simonides rules the country of Pentapolis which is 'our country of Greece'. Wilkins' novelisation of the play makes no mention of Greece at all, neither here nor elsewhere, and thereby avoids any attempt to place the location of Pentapolis in relation to Greece. The problem that I am about to investigate, then, is a peculiarity of the play. The dramatists apparently accept and the audience hears the form of the name as Greek, the country of five cities or, if the city is the country, the five-gated city or something similar. McJannet proposes that the name has been derived from the group of five cities on the northern coast of the Aegean whose names end in '-polis', names Shakespeare might have seen on a map of the journeys of St Paul, whose travels are in complex ways echoed in this play, a map which he would have found in Abraham Ortelius' magnificent atlas, *Theatrum Orbis Terrarum*, first published in 1570 and frequently reprinted thereafter, one of the many atlases that was itself the form of theatre best known to those early modern Londoners who frequented playhouses like the Globe.[5]

The word 'Greece' has already been spoken in the play. When Pericles, in flight from Tyre, arrives in Tarsus for the first time, the city is in the grip of famine. The arrival of Pericles's ship appears to be a threat but Pericles has had the ships display white flags, already a symbol of peacefulness, and on landing he quickly reassures Cleon 'Let not our ships and number of our men / Be like a beacon fired t'amaze your eyes' (1.4.84-5). The beacon was a sign of impending danger (like the beacons that had been lit along the coast to warn the country of the arrival of the Spanish Armada in 1588) but it was also by the 1590s a light on a coast to help ships steer at night. Pericles' image rather beautifully reverses the effect: the ship is the beacon warning the land. As A.F. Falconer points out in his fine study *Shakespeare and the Sea* (1964), Pericles' ships are acting as what was known as succour ships, ships loaded with food not arms[6]:

> …these our ships, you happily may think
> Are like the Trojan horse was stuffed within
> With bloody veins expecting overthrow,
> Are stored with corn to make your needy bread,
> And give them life whom hunger starved half dead. (1.4.90-4)

And the people of Tarsus, led by Cleon, respond 'The gods of Greece protect you' (95). Cleon, the Lord Governor of Tarsus, is then part of Greek colonial power: Tarsus may be in Asia, on the southern coast of what is now Turkey, but it is Greek in religion and civil authority, linked to the country where Simonides rules.

Could Pentapolis, like Tarsus, be part of the Greek Empire? If one looks at modern maps representing the travels of Apollonius of Tyre, the journeyer whose narrative underpins *Pericles*,[7] on such maps Pentapolis is not in Greece at all but in North Africa, further along the coast from where Apollonius at one point journeys to and from Egypt. As far as I can establish – and the problem of working it out is necessarily a remarkably difficult one – Shakespeare is the first person to move Pentapolis to Greece.[8] He may perhaps have been mistaken, affected by the nature of the name (his small Latin and less Greek sufficient to recognize the words that make up the name), but it seems to me more likely that he made the move because his map for the action of his narrative, his dramatized version of the story, could be heard by the audience as being fixed on the northern and eastern shores of the Mediterranean, wanting this particular account of cruising to be organized without a far-distant stop in the part of North Africa where the Apollonius story placed Pentapolis nor including a stop for Apollonius-Pericles in Egypt, tightening the sphere of journeying to an area marked at its western extremity by Pentapolis in Greece and at its southern extremity by Tyre.

Some editors are not sure where Pentapolis is. Roger Warren, for instance, glossing the fisherman's line, comments:

> Pentapolis is in fact 'a country of Africa consisting of five cities' (Steevens), though the dramatist clearly imagines that it is in Greece. (n. to 5.104, p.123)

But his 'Map showing the principal locations of *Pericles*' (p.10) shows it in its pre-*Pericles* position in North Africa. Wherever Pentapolis is 'in fact', the play's location is, in his view, in Greece. We may wonder, at this point, what an audience might have thought, whatever the dramatist might have imagined. Most of those for whom the geography of the play's source was an unknown mapping must, surely, have heard the dialogue to be placing Pentapolis in Greece. Those whose geography was better-educated and those who knew the Apollonius story well might have expected Simonides to be ruling in North Africa. For them, the fisherman's phrase 'our country of Greece' would have given a different valency to 'of', not a sense of naming (i.e. that 'our country of Greece' = 'Greece') but of possession ('our country of Greece' = 'our country that belongs to Greece').

Gossett's scholarship of early modern mapping goes beyond Warren's at this point but the result is similar. Her note reads:

> The authors could have known the North African location of Pentapolis from the 'Nomenclator Ptolemaicus' in Ortelius's 1595 *Theatrum Orbis Terrarum*. Nevertheless, the imaginative geography of the play confines it entirely to

coastal cities of the north-eastern Mediterranean basin, from Tyre in Asia Minor to an indeterminate location in Greece for Simonides' kingdom.

As her introduction shows, the maps in Ortelius include most of the play's locations except for Pentapolis, only the 'Nomenclator' including it in North Africa, but the map places Cyrene in North Africa and the *Historia Apolloni* has the Cleon character 'urge Pericles to sail to *Pentapolitanas Cyrenaeorum terras*' so that 'it appears that Pentapolis was equated with Cyrene, chief town of Cyrenaica, the province' (p.129).

Gossett knows that this might conflict with the fisherman's statement. She also knows that it is in direct conflict with a clear piece of meteorology and geography in *Pericles*. Marina states to Leonine that 'When I was born the wind was north' (4.1.50) and a north wind cannot blow a ship traveling from North Africa to somewhere close to Tarsus, i.e. the southern coast of Turkey. It is a navigational impossibility. There were, as Gossett points out, seven cities called Pentapolis and either the one on Cnidus, an island near Rhodes, or the one now called Tomi in Thrace would allow the journey to take place as Marina's definition of the wind suggests.[9] But, since 'Cyrene was the chief Hellenic colony in Africa', Gossett hears 'our country of Greece' as 'most easily understood as referring generally to the Greek or Hellenistic world, including the North African but Greek-named city of Pentapolis' (p.129). In this version, the memory of the source-narrative overrides in the audience's mind their knowledge of the effects of wind-direction on a crucial journey in the play. The view of the educated audience thus dominates any other possibility and the play's geography is supposed to be secured by tradition external to the play rather than by the play's clear statement about the weather.

One of the things that Shakespeare does in the late plays is to make his changes of location both rather effective and uncharacteristically careful. This is, after all, the man whose European geography was and would be prone to be a bit hazy from the surprising waterways that link Verona and Milan in *The Two Gentlemen of Verona* to the sea-coast of Bohemia in a play he would shortly be writing, *A Winter's Tale*. I have elsewhere explored the thoughtful geography of *Cymbeline*.[10] But there is, I suspect, a further reason why Shakespeare adjusts the geography of the Mediterranean in *Pericles*, moving Pentapolis from one country to another. If in *Pericles* Pentapolis were in North Africa, it would make it even less likely that if you were travelling from Pentapolis to Tyre you could in bad weather decide to stop off in Tarsus instead and leave your daughter there for the next 14 years or so. Whatever route you took from one city to the other in the Apollonius narrative would not possibly take you anywhere near Tarsus, whatever the weather.

The Apollonius narrative is of course really the Pericles narrative – or more accurately the Pericles narrative is really the Apollonius one. Only the names have been changed. For Shakespeare's appears to be the first of the myriad versions of the Apollonius story in which the hero's name is changed. There are so many versions of this story that saying that Shakespeare was the first has to be qualified with a phrase like 'as far as anyone knows' but Archibald's study with its extensive documentation of versions in Latin and the European vernacular languages up to 1609 treats Pericles as an invention for this play. Why then was the name Pericles chosen? It has been suggested that Shakespeare changed the name because Apollonius does not fit verse terribly easily. But neither Gower nor Chaucer, who mentions Apollonius in *The Canterbury Tales*, seems to have had any problem.[11]

I am not convinced either that Shakespeare is thinking of the Athenian statesman, even though he would have read the life of Pericles in North's Plutarch and though Wilkins had translated long sections concerning Pericles, 'a man of tried vertue and experience' in book 3 of *The History of Justine* (1606),[12] Beyond the fact that both Pericleses share certain qualities of statesmanliness they have almost nothing else to link them together. There is the story of the Athenian statesman having 'despaired for a time after the death of his only legitimate son'[13] and having to be won back to public life by Alcibiades but this seems a weak parallel: Pericles is grieving for Thaisa as well as Marina and, in any case, daughters are not sons.

Not much more convincing is the suggestion that the name derives from a close homophone, Pyrocles in Sidney's *Arcadia*. Both suffer shipwreck, like any number of characters in romance narratives; Pyrocles' friend Musidorus finds a suit of armour, as Pericles does; Pyrocles grieves for his apparently dead lover Philoclea and is rebuked for excessive grief by someone who turns out to be Philoclea herself. As Bullough wisely comments, 'Incidents such as these suggest that the tale of Apollonius of Tyre was one of the stories Sidney had in mind when writing his Arcadia. They do not prove that the dramatist was thinking of Sidney's romance'.

More likely is a kind of pun on the Latin word *periculum*, danger, for Pericles is recurrently in danger, either responding to it or encountering it. In some ways he is Shakespeare's 'danger man', and the nervy neurotic edge of TV's *Danger Man*, Patrick McGoohan, would serve the role of Pericles rather well. A character whose response to the news of his daughter's death is refusing to cut his hair and choosing to go into permanent mourning in a state of traumatized silence is not only taking grief far beyond the abnormal extremes of *Twelfth Night*'s Olivia but is also registering some kind of neurotic imbalance that will eventually need Marina's psychotherapeutic intervention. It is just possible that Shakespeare knew a version of the story that has not come down to us for in a French version known only in a manuscript now in Vienna Apollonius assumes as a false name 'Perillie', a name that also suggests his perils and perilousness, while in another French version the princess of Pentapolis 'writes to her father that she wants to marry "le perilliers de mer"'.[14] But he might also have known the rare words *periculous* and *periculousness* (derived, ultimately, from the familiar *perilous*), both of which *OED* lists as current in the mid-16th century.

To change the name from Apollonius was a radical act, a bit like renaming Oedipus Arthur but leaving the rest of the story intact. Indeed it may be more radical for the Apollonius narrative was more popular, better known even than the Oedipus myth. Over 114 manuscripts of the Latin narrative, the *Historia Apollonii Regis Tyri* survive, written between the ninth and the seventeenth centuries. Versions exist in France, Germany, Italy, Russia, Hungary, Bohemia, Norway, Iceland, Denmark, Holland and Spain. An oral folklorist collected a version in Greece in the early 20th century, over a thousand years after the story's earliest extant versions. In England it is the earliest known English romance and is almost certainly the only fictional narrative to survive in Old, Middle and Modern English versions. This is a genuinely pan-European narrative, a story whose presence across the whole of Europe is profound and pervasive. It is a story that is known, repeated, reworked, remembered, rethought but largely unaltered. Among the many versions Shakespeare did know or might have known we can count John Gower's in *Confessio Amantis* and a version by Lawrence Twine, *The Pattern of Painful Adventures*, published around 1594 and again in 1607 (but first entered in the Stationers' Register in 1574). Shakespeare had probably already used Gower's version and Twine's in writing the story of Egeon and the shipwreck in *The Comedy of Errors*. The narrative had been a part of the great collection known as the *Gesta Romanorum* (it was story 153 there) and that was probably where Twine found it but someone else who read it there was François de Belleforest who included it in his *Histoires Tragiques* (published in 1570 and 1595), a volume Shakespeare may well have known for its inclusion of a version of the Hamlet narrative that he seems to have used.

In 1608, the year before *Pericles* itself was first printed, a little novel appeared called *The Painful Adventures of Pericles Prince of Tyre*. Its title-page carries a woodblock showing John Gower because, as the title goes on to explain, this novel is 'The true history of the play of Pericles as it was lately presented by the worthy and ancient poet John Gower', while the argument ends 'Onely intreating the Reader to receive this Historie in the same maner as it was under the habite of ancient Gower the famous English Poet, by the Kings Majesties Players excellently presented'.[15]

The relation of play to novel is complex and vexed but there are two remarkable features in all this: the first is that of all the many versions of the Apollonian story *Pericles* is the first to turn it into drama and second is that Wilkins' little novel is the earliest example extant of what is now a common genre, the book of the film or, in this case, the book of the play, the turning of a play into a novel, changing its genre as a direct response to the success of the performed version, a sign that there is commercial profit to be made out of transferring across from stage-play to prose narrative.

Not only, then, is the narrative of Apollonius an old story, a familiar story, a European myth but it is also one that Shakespeare chooses to remind us is one we already know. What strikes me as most remarkable is that Shakespeare underlines from the very start that this is an old story, presented by an old poet in old-fashioned language, a diction consciously archaic to underline the point. Gower's opening lines emphasise different ways in which the story has been communicated:

> To sing a song that old was sung,
> From ashes ancient Gower is come,
> Assuming man's infirmities
> To glad your ear and please your eyes.
> It hath been sung at festivals,
> On ember eves and holy ales,
> And lords and ladies in their lives
> Have read it for restoratives.
> The purchase is to make men glorious,
> *Et bonum quo antiquius eo melius.* (1.0.1-10)

It has been sung (for poetry was seen as linked to music in its earliest forms) and it has been read. It has also, by implication, been listened to by many and read by a few. It is a narrative that belongs to everyone and that is, as the Latin tag makes clear, all the better for its age (the older a good thing is the better – to translate a little more accurately). Its age is a mark of its worth.

But Gower's lines do something else as well, linking the narrative explicitly to Christian ritual. This is not a holiday story but one for a holy-day, not only something one might listen to at a time when one is taking a break from work but also at a time which is a consecrated one. *OED* defines *holy-day* as 'A day consecrated or set apart for religious observance, usually in commemoration of some sacred person or event'. Is Apollonius some kind of sacred person? Is the play some kind of narrative of a saint's life? The 'festivals' where his story has been sung are, I take it, religious ones, not civic or secular. *Pericles* was one of the two Shakespeare plays (the other was *King Lear*) performed by the Catholic players who visited Gowthwaite Hall, the home of Sir John Yorke, in 1609.[16] It is a story for the solemn moment of ember-eves, one of 'the four periods of fasting and prayer…appointed by the Church to be observed respectively in the four seasons of the year' (*OED*). Ember-eve is the solemn vigil preceding an ember-day fast. And this story rightly belongs there, at a communal event of singing and listening (like the mass itself). Aristocrats may read it, but the community hears it sung. There is, of course, a subtext here: what we might call the sacred function of theatre, the careful alignment of the experience of watching *Pericles* and listening to it as analogous to the experience of a religious festival or holy-day. It is a bold claim but Gower becomes not only a function of the presence of the author – both an ancient poet and Shakespeare himself, for one narrator of the ancient story is much like another – but also a kind of priest controlling our experience of this sacred event, the mediator who makes us share the experience, participate in an event which, since its performance explicitly depends on our co-operation, the involvement of our imaginations, is, in the modern phrase, an interactive interface. The actors make the play happen, Gower makes the play happen and we make it happen. Without us it cannot work. When, later in the narrative, Gower wants to take us back to Tarsus with the older Pericles arriving to collect his grown-up daughter (only to be told that she is dead), he offers the following complex idea:

> Well-sailing ships and bounteous winds have brought
> This king to Tarsus – think his pilot thought;
> So with his steerage shall your thoughts groan –
> To fetch his daughter home, who first is gone. (4.4.17-20)[17]

It is our imagination that must steer the ship of the play, piloting it along, making sure it arrives safely. The lines suggest that it is Pericles's steerage that we must go with, our thinking accompanying his direction but also responsible for it. Pilots are, after all, crucially experienced navigators, people who know the dangers, especially the ones around the entrances of harbours and ports, the people who can bring the many ships of the play as well as the ship that is the play safely into the road, that 'sheltered piece of water near the shore where vessels may lie at anchor in safety', as the OED defines this meaning (road *n.* 3.a).

I want to go back to the *Historia Apollonii*, the Latin version of this story, for there when the Marina-figure (her name in the story is Tarsia) tries to break through the walls of Apollonius's grief she asks him a series of ten riddles, five of which are to do with the sea. Let me just note here that the narrative of the *Historia* is full of these kinds of structural echoes: just as it begins with Apollonius having to solve the riddle of Antiochus, the riddle of incest, so it will move towards this other set of riddles, the ones that will lead to a transforming, magical and entirely proper relationship of father to daughter. Shakespeare may choose to do without the second set of riddles but in what may be the play's greatest and most beautiful line, the echo of one evil form of family relationship is heard metamorphosed into the restorative, resurrecting one: 'Thou that beget'st him that did thee beget' (5.1.185). One of the ways in which a cruise like the journey of the play *Pericles* is organized is by structural repetition, echoes of earlier events, as each visit that a character makes to a place, each time he or she ends up in that particular harbour, reminds us of when the play was there before.

I did not see the last Royal Shakespeare Company production (2001, directed by Adrian Noble) in its London incarnation at the Roundhouse where it was played in a semi-promenade version. But I think *Pericles* is a natural for a full-scale promenade production in which the audience follow the characters to and fro across a playing-space that would be the map of the north-eastern part of the Mediterranean, in which the journeying of the characters and the action would also be the journeying of the audience as we see the action at a place that spatially represents its positioning, their journey as our journey, our thoughts piloting them around the theatre from port to port, sea-road to sea-road, stopping at the stations of the suffering that is the passion of Pericles.

Let me go back again to how you get from Pentapolis to Tyre via Tarsus. Apollonius set sail from Pentapolis in North Africa intending to go to Tyre. The *Historia Apollonii* is beautifully explicit about the weather and the sea: 'they set sail on a steady course with a following wind. For several days and nights they were detained on the wicked sea by various strong winds'.[18] His wife gives birth and appears to die and her coffined corpse is dumped in the sea from where it floats across to Ephesus and is cast up on the beach on the third day. After narrating the bringing back to life of Apollonius' wife, the first of the play's resurrections (the event whose echoes and repetitions are the most important that the action negotiates and organizes), the *Historia* moves back to consider what has happened to Apollonius himself: 'Meanwhile Apollonius had sailed on, in deep mourning. Steered by God, he arrived at Tarsus'.[19]

There is no dramatic scene here where in the middle of the storm, about to have his wife's corpse thrown overboard, Pericles resolves to change course for Tarsus, making a strong and sensible decision in the light of the imminent danger. Instead here Apollonius has no choice in the matter: 'gubernante deo', 'with god steering'. It seems the right kind of comment for a work that was 'sung at festivals / On ember eves and holy ales'. But it is part of Apollonius's world, not Pericles's. Whatever else we might think about who or what divine or human powers are in control at different points of the action of *Pericles*, at this point the difference is clear: Pericles makes his own destiny here, deciding where to go. It is not that the ship is somehow hundreds of miles off course in the storm and only through the grace of God does it end up safely somewhere, far from the course that the ship had been steered on by human agency. Instead there is a perfectly sensible reason for being close to Tarsus in the first place and here I go back to the rest of the note to 3.1.73 in the New Cambridge edition of the play:

> If Pentapolis is in Greece, as the play declares, a glance at the map…would suggest that any reasonable course from thence to Tyre would not go anywhere near Tarsus. However, Shakespeare probably had in mind the navigational customs of English seamen of the sixteenth century, whose practice was to steer from headland to headland, within sight of land; this coastal navigation was known at the time as 'pilotage'. It is therefore quite possible that Shakespeare imagined Pericles' ship sailing to the north of Cyprus, rather than the south.

DelVecchio and Hammond are more or less right but I need to outline early modern systems of navigation. The early modern world distinguished between navigation and pilotage. Navigation, as Dr John Dee commented in his Elizabethan notes on the problem, 'demonstrateth how by the shortest way, and in the shortest time, a sufficient ship…be conducted'.[20] By the 1580s, in Michiel Coignet's Flemish manual, the distinction is fixed between this mode (which needed the assistance of complex instruments and a substantial knowledge of astronomy and cosmography) and which he called 'grand navigation' and what Coignet called 'common navigation' and defined as follows:

> The whole science of common navigation is nothing more than knowing perfectly by sight all capes, ports and rivers, how they appear by sea, what distance lies between them, and what is the course from one to another; also, in knowing the bearing of the moon on which high and low tides occur, the ebb and flow of the waters, the depth, and the nature of the bottom.[21]

'Nothing more than' all that. But this is pragmatic local knowledge, empirical observation, learned by experience; there is no theory here, only a practice. You translated what you had seen into knowledge. You had seen the capes and steered by them or you followed others' reports of their observations – even the crude woodcuts in Pierre Garcie's early-16th century books would be amply sufficient for that. Indeed, a ship's course was called its caping; to cape was 'to keep a course' (*OED* cape v.[1]). For coastal sailing, distances were measured in kennings, a rough measure equivalent to the distance you could see while at sea, approximately 21 miles or 34 kilometres,[22] or, to be a little more precise, the distance you would be from a headland and still just keep it in sight from the masthead.

Of course this kind of practical information could easily be written down. In the Mediterranean world it soon was, built up from pilots' private notebooks into manuals known in Italian as 'portolani'. *Portolani* told you how to travel safely along the coast from place to place and they were built up into a comprehensive book of instructions for the whole of the Mediterranean and the Black Sea, known as the *Compasso da navigare*. It contained bearings, distances in miles, descriptions of landmarks and dangerous areas, instructions for safe entries to harbours and information about depths and anchorages. *Portolani* also, strikingly, included some open-sea crossings, some pieces of what Coignet called 'grand navigation' which also made use of astronomy and cosmography, to travel between capes and islands of anything up to 800 miles in distance.

It was different for English sailors and others piloting in northern Europe. They used what were called *routiers*, or in English 'rutters'. Rutters stuck to the coasts, except for the journey from Gibraltar to the Channel, and for a long time, till the early 16th century, they still measured distances in kennings, not miles. But they gave far more detailed accounts than their Mediterranean equivalents of soundings of depths and bottoms along long stretches of coastline. They were also far more concerned about tides (hardly a problem in the Mediterranean unless you were close to the Straits of Messina). Printed rutters included complex details about ports and diagrammatic tables of tides (because if you got a tide wrong you might well run aground even in a familiar harbour).

If in the Mediterranean you sailed out of sight of land you had to keep a dead-reckoning, working out where you were by taking a bearing, calculating your speed and correcting for crosswinds and currents. Taking a bearing was easy, though unfavourable winds meant that sticking to it was difficult – the traverse board enabled the helmsman to keep track of tacking in relation to time reasonably efficiently by marking on a compass rose one peg for direction for each half-hour of a watch. Once the log was invented in the late-16th century, it was not too difficult to work out your speed, though calculating time accurately at sea was still a problem. Put it all together and you have a remarkable number of elements that are likely to be in error: grand navigation was not quite hit-or-miss but it was certainly liable to land you somewhere rather different from where you thought you were: many mariners must have had to ask versions of Viola's 'What country, friends, is this?' and it is no surprise that the shipwrecked Pericles of Act 2 really has no idea where he has been washed ashore.

As well as the manuals, the portolani and rutters, there were charts for navigation and pilotage. Older English seamen were suspicious of charts. William Bourne who published (in 1574) the first major manual of seamanship in English, *A Regiment for the Sea*, noted the problem: 'I have knowen within this 20 years, that them that wer aunciet masters of shippes hath derided and mocked them that have occupied their cards and plattes…saying: that they care not for their sheepes skins, for he could keep a better account upon a boord'.[23] Charts were fairly inaccurate: they took no account of the fact that the earth was round. All lines pointing to magnetic north were vertical and parallel. This did not matter much in the Mediterranean because the changes in latitude were small but it would in the north, in the seas around England. But the charts were not primarily intended to enable one to set a course in that sense. They showed coastlines with remarkable detail and accuracy; they marked hundreds of names of places and coastal features along the coasts in black with important harbours in red; they showed virtually nothing inland apart from major rivers and mountains visible from the sea. And the sea itself is crossed with hundreds of lines showing the directions one should take, the course one should bear, between different places, lines of constant bearing that would, with good fortune and decent weather and nothing much to push one off course, take one on a navigational rather than pilotage route.

Shakespeare's representations of sailing, navigation and their consequences are mostly set in the Mediterranean. Think of the storm in *The Tempest* that blows off course the fleet traveling from Tunis to Naples. Think of Viola and Sebastian shipwrecked off the coast of Illyria, roughly where Yugoslavia used to be. Think above all of Pericles to-ing and fro-ing across the north-eastern Mediterranean across many years of travelling, a whole series of journeys between these points, trying to find someone or trying to be lost, trying by turns to connect or disconnect himself from the structures of power, of community, of responsibility, of family and of social or human contact. When grief leads him towards mutism and a noticeable reluctance to visit the barber's, he takes to the sea, wandering across his part of the world ceaselessly, a self-driven Flying Dutchman, forcing himself to roam the seas until redeemed by love. By turns working along coasts (caping and pilotage) or following those invisible roads that mark the tracks of navigational journeying along such well-travelled seas, Pericles charts a series of kinds of journeys: travel towards or away from or, most piteously, journeys that take you nowhere, that are simply acts of being permanently in transit, unsettled, unplaced, displaced, denying belonging.

It is also a journey clearly marked by the edges he touches on. This is a play which speaks the words *shore* and *shores* eighteen times and *coast* six more. Hence Pericles 'By waves from coast to coast is tossed' (2.0.34), while 'The seas.../Washed me from shore to shore' (2.1.5-6). The word *shore* is repeatedly linked to being 'cast upon' it or 'tossed up' on it or 'driven upon' it: see, for example, 2.3.82, 2.3.86, 3.2.50 and 3.2.55, all examples of the violent disgorging of what the sea discards. The shores can turn into other senses too: the 'common shores of filth' (4.5.178) of which Marina speaks, shores that are the part of the foreshore used by everyone for their rubbish which the tides will wash off; and, most movingly, the shores can mark the edges and limits of existence itself, the fragile borders of the body of which, at the extreme moment of reunion with Marina, Pericles is suddenly aware:

> Give me a gash, put me to present pain,
> Lest this great sea of joys rushing upon me
> O'erbear the shores of my mortality
> And drown me with their sweetness. (5.1.181-4)

But this is also the consequence of reunion with an individual who comes neither from nation (one sense of *shores*) nor from the land itself, belonging to no shore at all:

> *Pericles.*   what countrywoman?
>   Here of these shores?
> *Marina.*   No, nor of any shores. (5.1.93-4)

The person who has been coasting through so much of the play encounters the person who is always a stranger: 'Where do you live?' 'Where I am but a stranger' (5.1.104-5). The coasts and shores of journeying meet their own impossibility, that of never having arrived, and only then can they move towards their final terminus, the reunions and the play's end.

But I want to suggest something else as well about the nature of the play itself. Rutters and portolani, charts and tables were the product of what was known, seen, understood. They turn accumulated empirical observation into a guide for others. They move between what is controllable as data through eyesight (the markings of the coast) and firm knowledge (the effects of local tides) and what is awkwardly and at times dangerously uncontrollable: journeys through open sea with vulnerable instruments. They teeter between the known and the unknown, the safe and the fraught, the manageable and the temptingly but terrifyingly unmanageable. *Pericles* itself is a journey across the mappings of narrative represented by the Apollonius story, not only the *Historia Apollonii* itself but all its manifestations, all those features of every version of it that are like each other or deliberately or accidentally unlike, between the known and the unknown, the familiar and the original. Shakespeare turns the Apollonius narrative into the drama of Pericles, creating that particularly complex awareness of the transition into action to which Gower repeatedly draws our attention. To use the two kinds of navigation that I have described, I would want to say that the narrative is in one sense so familiar, so known, as to be a kind of rutter or portolano, while the drama is so unfamiliar as a form that it represents grand navigation, open-seas journeying, not just across a space as familiar, as little prone to error as the Mediterranean, but across a tract of water as vast as the Atlantic, on the other side of which you have no idea what country you will land on. Gower's version or Twine's or the anonymous author of the *Historia Apollonii* all included passages in dialogue but these are bits of conversation in a narrative, not the fundamental form of event in spoken drama, the dialogue without which the play cannot proceed as drama.

Wilkins' novel included plenty of snatches of dialogue as well, some of which are clearly written in blank verse, though printed in prose in the volume. Indeed, given the difficulties and corruptions that many editors have found in the first quarto of the play, our only textual authority, our Gower, there has been a temptation to work from Wilkins' novel and dramatise speeches and scenes that are not in the quarto at all; Gary Taylor and Mac Jackson did that most comprehensively for the Oxford *Complete Works*, acting as dramatists confronted with a prose narrative, recapitulating the experience of Shakespeare in confronting Twine and Gower. But if the Wilkins novel is some version of the play, it is at the same time not a play; it is a prose narrative, not a drama.

But then, and here is the point, the play is not fully a drama either, caught between enacting and narrating, making Gower as much our pilot as our thoughts are. When actions 'Are brought your eyes', they act, as Gower says, as 'tidings to the contrary' ('But tidings to the contrary / Are brought your eyes', 2.0.14-15) and in that case, he adds, 'what need speak I?' What need indeed? Drama denies the narrator, displaces him. Later, confronted with what is about to happen in the storm in which Marina is born, Gower offers a self-enacting event:

> And what ensues in this fell storm
> Shall for itself itself perform.
> I nill relate, action may
> Conveniently the rest convey,
> Which might not what by me is told. (3.0.53-7)

Gower is a narrator who, as he identifies, 'stands i'th'gaps' (4.4.8), marking the interstices, those connections which drama does not, sometimes cannot and occasionally refuses to show – hence for instance the way in which Wilkins' novel, but not the play, narrates how Antiochus seduced his daughter, something the play treats as an event in the past, of no importance to the dramatized narrative of Pericles himself.

After Gower has narrated the first storm and its shipwreck – repeated storms are another part of the structure of repetition that organizes this play's Mediterranean cruise, the disruptive events that stop the predictability of journeying – he announces the entrance of Pericles: 'And here he comes' but Gower's line and a half after that, what the French rule-makers for neo-classical drama would call the *liaison de vue*, the connection of sight, are, for me, crucial: 'And here he comes. What shall be next, / Pardon old Gower, this 'longs the text' (2.0.39-40). The understanding of the passage depends on the ambiguity of *'longs* (Q's 'long's'). It may be heard as meaning 'belongs', what now happens belongs to the definition of 'text' as drama, not narrative, as play to be shown and not poem to be heard. But Gower's interventions also lengthen the whole performance-text, of which they are a part, if we take the other sense that *'longs* has here. In belonging to the text of *Pericles* Gower's choruses join it together, acting as dramatic stitching to make the drama a web of lines radiating across the map of the Apollonius narrative like the lines on the early charts that link harbours and headlands. But the entrance of Pericles is also a 'this' that belongs to the text, the different text of drama, not the text of narration.

In a way that no previous version of this story had had to do, the author or authors of *Pericles* have to make acts of division precisely because he or they are play-makers, creators of the wrought artefact that a playwright makes. They separate narration from action, story-telling from story-showing, turning the narrator into an actor, the author into a performer in 'the text' they have made. As the play safely reaches its magnificent conclusions, both the reunion of Pericles and his daughter in spoken language and the reunion of Pericles and his wife more in sight than sound, so the play shows that, if you can't always get there starting from here, Shakespeare can pilot you here, caping the headlands of the narrative but also moving and displacing once-familiar identifying features, remapping the territory and occasionally, as in the reunions, striking out in grand navigational gestures across unmapped territory to create the exhilarating immediacy of the here of drama, starting from the there of the old story.

Notes

[1] Unless otherwise indicated all quotations from the play are taken from Suzanne Gossett's excellent edition for the Arden Shakespeare 3rd series (London: Thomson Learning, 2004), here 1.2.61. *Pericles*, which has not had a major edition since Philip Edwards' New Penguin version of 1976, has now benefited from three important contributions: Doreen DelVecchio and Antony Hammond's deeply conservative treatment of Q1 in their New Cambridge Shakespeare version (Cambridge: Cambridge University Press, 1998), Gossett's measured and inventive Arden and Roger Warren's Oxford edition, probably the one most sensitive to the play in performance but based on the reconstructed text created by Gary Taylor and MacDonald P. Jackson for the Oxford *Complete Works* (edited by Stanley Wells, Gary Taylor and others [Oxford: The Clarendon Press, 1986]), extensively using the novella by George Wilkins, *The Painful Adventures of Pericles Prince of Tyre* (1608), a prose version, 'Being the true History of the Play of *Pericles*, as it was lately presented by the worthy and ancient Poet John Gower', to supplement what are perceived as lacunae and errors in the text (Oxford: The Clarendon Press, 2003). Quotations from Wilkins are taken from Geoffrey Bullough's edition in *Narrative and Dramatic Sources of Shakespeare* vol. 6 (1966), as reproduced on the *Arden Shakespeare* cd-rom.

[2] See, e.g., Warren, p.10; DelVecchio and Hammond, p.xiv; Gossett, p.130.

[3] See, for example, John Gillies, *Shakespeare and the Geography of Difference*, (Cambridge: Cambridge University Press, 1994); John Gillies and Virginia Mason Vaughan, eds., *Playing the Globe: Genre and Geography in English Renaissance Drama* (Madison: Fairleigh Dickinson Press, 1998); Garrett A. Sullivan, Jr., *The Drama of Landscape* (Stanford: Stanford University Press, 1998); Andrew Gordon and Bernhard Klein, eds., *Literature, Mapping, and the Politics of Space in Early Modern Britain* (Cambridge: Cambridge University Press, 2001); and Bernhard Klein, *Maps and the Writing of Space in Early Modern England and Ireland* (Basingstoke: Palgrave, 2001).

[4] But see Linda McJannet, 'Genre and Geography: the Eastern Mediterranean in *Pericles* and *The Comedy of Errors*' in Gillies and Vaughan, pp. 86-106.

5 McJannet, pp.91-2.
6 Lieutenant-Commander Alexander Frederick Falconer, V.R.D., M.A., *Shakespeare and the Sea* (New York: Frederick Ungar Publishing Co., 1964), pp.26-7. If the index entries are a reasonable guide, *Pericles* appears in Falconer's book more often than any other play.
7 See, most significantly, in Elizabeth Archibald's major study of the material, *Apollonius of Tyre: Medieval and Renaissance Themes and Variations* (Woodbridge: D.S.Brewer, 1991), where the map appears on the endpapers.
8 There are, of course, difficulties caused by the collaborative process between Shakespeare and George Wilkins in the writing of this play in identifying the dramatist of this or any other moment of the play simply as Shakespeare. My point here does not depend on which of the two was responsible for the shift and occasionally in this article I have found it easier to refer to the 'author' as 'Shakespeare' rather than as 'Shakespeare and/or Wilkins'. On the collaboration see MacDonald P. Jackson, *Defining Shakespeare: 'Pericles' as Test Case* (Oxford: Oxford University Press, 2003) and Brian Vickers, *Shakespeare, Co-Author* (Oxford, Oxford University Press, 2002), pp.291-332.
9 I ignore here the possibility that Marina is mistaken about the wind's direction – that way madness lies.
10 See 'Staging Shakespeare in Europe' in Ladina Bezzola Lambert and Balz Engler, eds., *Shifting the Scene: Shakespeare in European Culture* (Newark: University of Delaware Press, 2004), pp.21-40.
11 To be strictly accurate, Gower names him Appolinus which is marginally easier metrically.
12 See Gossett, p.168.
13 Archibald, p.215.
14 Ibid.
15 For the text, see Bullough.
16 On this extraordinary event, see C.J.Sisson, 'Shakespeare Quartos as Prompt-Copies with some account of Cholmeley's Players and a New Shakespeare Allusion' *RES* 48 (1942), pp.129-43; G.W.Boddy, 'Players of Interludes in North Yorkshire in the Early Seventeenth Century' Repaginated offprint from North Yorkshire County Record Office Publications no.7, Journal 3, April 1976; John L.Murphy, *Darkness and Devils: Exorcism and 'King Lear'* (Athens, Ohio, Ohio University Press, 1984), pp.93-118; Phebe Jensen, 'Recusancy, Festivity and Community: The Simpsons at Gowlthwaite [sic] Hall', *Reformation* 6 (2002), pp.75-102.
17 Though I usually quote Gossett, here I do not agree with her emendation of Q's 'sterage' to 'sternage' (an unnecessary complication) nor, following Malone, her change of Q's 'grone' to 'go on', giving the excessively weak rhyme 'go on/gone'. The idea of thoughts groaning makes good sense to me and the idea of following painfully his course, 'steerage', is both simple and enticing.
18 Archibald, pp. 137-8.

[19] Archibald, p.143.
[20] Quoted by J.H. Parry, *The Age of Reconnaissance* (2nd ed., Berkeley: University of California Press, 1981), p.83. In addition to Parry's outstanding study, particularly, Part 1 'The Conditions for Discovery', I have also found helpful David W. Waters' massive study, *The Art of Navigation in England in Elizabethan and Early Stuart Times* (New Haven: Yale University Press, 1958) and two important editions of early texts: E.G.R. Taylor's edition of William Bourne's *A Regiment for the Sea* (1574) and other writings (Cambridge: Cambridge University Press for the Hakluyt Society, 1963); and Waters's *The Rutters of the Sea: The Sailing Directions of Pierre Garcie* (New Haven: Yale University Press, 1967), a facsimile edition of early French and English rutters, including Pierre Garcie's *Le Routier de la mer* (published between 1502 and 1520), his *Le grant routier* (2nd ed., 1521) and Robert Copland's translation (first published 1528, facsimile of 1557 [?] edition) as *The Rutter of the See*. In connection with the naming of Pericles it may be worth noting that Garcie's foreword to *Le grant routier* speaks of 'les grans perilz et dangiers qui sont es ondes & gouffres marins' and of 'les…miserables perilz de la mer vehemête' (quoted Waters, *The Rutters of the See*, p.3).
[21] Quoted in Parry, p.83.
[22] See Waters, *The Rutters of the Sea*, p.23.
[23] Quoted in Parry, p.100.

MIDSUMMER METADRAMA:
'PYRAMUS AND THISBE' AND EARLY ENGLISH HOUSEHOLD THEATRE

Tom Pettitt

More actively and variously engaged in his theatre than any contemporary, it is hardly surprising that Shakespeare needed to express himself on a dramatic art which was undergoing extraordinary and revolutionary development. But while other player-playwrights like Jonson and Heywood also pursued such discussions externally to their dramatic production, Shakespeare's are exclusively embedded within his plays themselves, contributing significantly to their characteristic metadramatic quality. Most of Shakespeare's plays are essays on drama, and by a well-qualified authority. But the perspective can also be reversed: the metadramatic features provide significant interpretative access to the plays in which they occur, be they explicit invocations or the actual production of dramatic activities, or action implicitly but plausibly analogous to drama.

With *Hamlet* as its only near rival, *A Midsummer Night's Dream* is Shakespeare's most sustained and intense piece of metadramatic writing. For all its imperfections and disruptions its play-within-the-play, unlike 'The Murder of Gonzago,' is complete. 'Pyramus and Thisbe' is prefaced short-term by the stage audience's discussion of its suitability and likely quality, long-term by the revealing rehearsal scenes. It is punctuated by the comments of audience and performers, and followed by an authoritative assessment from its chief spectator. And this occurs in the highly congenial environment of a host play whose human characters enter a wood which becomes a stage on which literally to rehearse (3.1.3-5) or metaphorically to be directed in a 'fond pageant' (3.2.114), by a 'king of shadows' (3.2.347).[1]

The present study will not find space to discuss the familiar metadramatic connections between 'Pyramus and Thisbe' and *Romeo and Juliet*, the style of dramatic writing in the generation before Shakespeare, or contemporary debates on the nature of dramatic illusion,[2] and I have explored elsewhere how in rehearsal and performance 'Pyramus and Thisbe' is subjected to the same kind of deliberate revisions and contextual pressures which will have affected Shakespeare's own plays on their trajectory from page to stage, and which may have produced the textual characteristics it shares with some of the Elizabethan 'bad' quartos.[3] What follows will rather assess how appreciation of *A Midsummer Night's Dream* may be enhanced by correctly identifying the Elizabethan connotations of the context and form of its play-within-the-play.

The Athenian Nuptials

'Pyramus and Thisbe' is performed at the wedding revels of an aristocratic household, the host play going out of its way to insist and elaborate on these auspices. Duke Theseus and his bride have returned from the wedding ceremony, together with the two young couples who – after the adolescent fuss and bother which constitutes their romantic comedy – have joined them at the altar. Theseus now calls for 'revels' (5.1.36) to pass the time between the dessert or 'after-supper' which concluded their banquet, and bed-time (5.1.34), be it 'masques ... dances' (5.1.32), 'music' (5.1.40), or a 'play' (5.1.36).

Most of the items on the list duly proffered seem more pseudo-classical than Elizabethan in both content and performance mode, which may be why they are rejected in favour of 'A tedious brief scene of young Pyramus / And his love Thisbe' (5.1.56-57), which will prove more familiar to the theatre audience. It is to be performed by 'Hard-handed men that work in Athens here' (5.1.72) whom we have met earlier – '.... *Quince the carpenter, and Snug the joiner, and Bottom the weaver, and Flute the bellows-mender, and Snout the tinker, and Starveling the tailor*' (1.2.0.SD) – when they assembled with the express purpose of preparing to perform 'before the Duke and Duchess on his wedding day at night' (1.2.6-7). When Bottom addresses them as 'masters' (1.2.15) he is probably specifying their technical qualifications and status within their respective crafts, and thus their substance and standing within the civic community, however much they will later be ridiculed or patronised at court. The dismissive 'rude mechanicals' preferred in criticism is actually Puck's (3.2.9): it is at least more accurate and charitable than Andrew Weiner's 'churls.'[4]

It is also vital to appreciate that what the Athenian craftsmen perform for their lord involves more than 'Pyramus and Thisbe.' Perceived as performance rather than text, their offering constitutes three distinct parts. Heralded (in the Folio text) by a flourish of trumpets (5.1.107.SD) Quince advances to preside over a substantial Presentation, starting with the prologue-proper, which, disencumbered of Quince's mis-punctuation, would have done well enough by way of ingratiating the company with the audience and announcing the beginning of the performance. (1.2.108-117). There follows a spectacular processional entry of all the characters, in costume, led (again courtesy of a Folio stage direction) by a trumpeter (5.1.125.SD). Quince's 'Gentles, perchance you wonder at this show' (5.1.126) refers to this, rather than a dumb show, of which the text has no indication. On the other hand it is quite possible that as he proceeds to present the characters individually, and particularly when he elaborates on their roles:

> This grizly beast, which 'Lion' hight by name,
> The trusty Thisbe coming first by night
> Did scare away ... (5.1.138-140),

the performers make at least some token gesture towards acting it out.

We might distinguish the second item, 'Pyramus and Thisbe' itself, as the play-proper, but the performers supply the Elizabethan term 'interlude' (1.2.5; 5.1.154), which early usage indeed associates with plays performed under festive (usually household) auspices. Disregarding Shakespeare's various satirical agendas, its most distinctive feature is the very mixed dramaturgy. A basically representational approach (evidenced by the fear the lion will frighten the ladies), is compromised by moments in a presentational mode more appropriate to the semi-dramatic items on each side of it, as if it were dramaturgically contaminated by the context. Thus just as (and even though) all the characters are introduced to the audience in the Presentation, several of them do so themselves in the interlude: 'In this same interlude it doth befall / That I, one Snout by name, present a wall' (5.1.154-55; cf. 5.1.217ff.; 235ff.).

When the interlude has stumbled to its melodramatic conclusion, there follows 'a bergamask dance between two of our company' (5.1.346). Textually insignificant (it evidently occurs between 5.1.353 and 354), as performance it will doubtless have involved a significant degree of action and spectacle, and have taken some time. The bergamask seems originally to have been an Italian folk tradition, popularised by the *commedia dell'arte,* and probably involved mimetic action, most likely on a wooing motif.[5] Given the use of masks signalled by the name we may designate this final item in the three-part show the masking.[6]

English Household Theatre

Categorizing the show of the Athenian craftsmen in terms of Elizabethan theatre and drama has more than antiquarian perspectives, for the way an audience identifies it will have a significant impact on their understanding of the play which (more or less) culminates with it. This may indeed, as Louis Montrose asserts, be 'Shakespeare's comic representation of civic, artisanal culture and its relationship to the state'[7] but its implications will depend on just what sort of theatre and relationship is being depicted. The task involves an excursion into as yet poorly mapped territory on the borders between the stage, pageantry and seasonal custom: authoritative statements that 'Pyramus and Thisbe' is some kind of antimasque, or a jig, need not be accepted without further consideration.[8]

As an amateur production, it would be natural to relate the mechanicals' performance to English drama prior to or independent of the commercialisation of the preceding generation, and this, not least when performed by urban craftsmen, is conventionally taken as synonymous with the mystery cycles. The latter persisted in many places into the post-medieval period, and as often noted the young Shakespeare could very well have seen the mysteries at nearby Coventry, whose last performance was in 1576. Linking 'Pyramus and Thisbe' to the mystery cycles[9] in turn facilitates and encourages discussion of the degree to which *A Midsummer Night's Dream* is somehow about the transition from the medieval civic theatre, and community culture, represented by the mystery cycles, to the early-modern commercial spirit, in league with the royal court, of the Elizabethan popular theatre.[10]

Shakespeare's craftsmen come closest to their cousins of Coventry, York, Chester and Wakefield with Quince's explanation at their first meeting that those assembled have been chosen from amongst their fellow townsmen as being 'fit ... to play' (1.2.5), very much in the spirit of the 1476 York ordinance directing the organizers of the mystery cycle there to select performers 'as they shall fynde sufficant in persoune and Conyng.[11] Otherwise it is hard to imagine productions more dissimilar than 'Pyramus and Thisbe' and the mystery cycles, which were anyway far from being the only or the most typical form of late-medieval community theatre. Peter Holland's claim that we lack evidence 'for the kind of performance by workers at an aristocratic celebration that takes place in *A Midsummer Night's Dream*' is correct only with regard to the Ovidian content:[12]

The mechanicals' show, precisely when seen as a whole, and in context, can be identified with a tradition of theatre which is adequately documented, if poorly represented by surviving texts, and characterized by a customary encounter between community performers on the one side and noble spectators on the other.[13] In this it may be analogous to the pageantry put on when the royal household visited communities on progresses, and which is often appealed to in this respect,[14] but in theatrical terms the tradition reproduced in Shakespeare's play is the reverse of this: the visit of community representatives to the noble household.

When a household of some social significance engaged in revels – typically during the Christmas to Twelfth Night season – men from local communities came to the 'great house' to perform before the household and its guests, the largesse or refreshment with which they were duly rewarded conveniently creating our surviving documentation. A classic instance, from a period well before the decline of the mystery cycles, is the Household Account Book of Richard Beauchamp, Earl of Warwick, which for the winter revels season of 1420-21 records payments to 'six ... from Slimbridge... playing [*ludentibus*] before the lady' (the Earl himself was away in France rehearsing for *1 Henry VI*), and 'four from Wotton' similarly 'playing': both communities (four and five miles, respectively, from Berkeley Castle, the Warwick residence) comprised dependents (including tenants) of the Earl of Warwick.[15] Chronologically closer is the 1551 expenditure on feeding 'four singers and players' from nearby Margaretting at Christmastide in the household of Sir William Petre at Ingatestone,[16] and that such customary visits continued through and beyond the Shakespearean period is indicated by analogous payments to 'players' from Downham (12 miles), Ribchester (9 miles), Clitheroe (9 miles), Whalley (5 miles) and Burnley (8 miles) for Christmas-season performances before the household of Thomas Walmesley of Dunkelhalgh, Lancashire, in the 1620's and 1630's.[17]

The traditional rewards for such performances were a far cry from the 'sixpence a day during his life' (4.2.18-19) Flute reckons Bottom could have got from the Duke, but Flute may have envisaged Bottom being taken on as a part-time household player: Peter Greenfield has suggested that such customary, courtesy visits might have led to the development of semi-professional acting companies, precursors of the common players.[18] Be that as it may, they were effectively demonstrations of interdependence and reciprocal interests, and historicist approaches may overstress the exceptional nature or the confrontational perspectives of the presence of the mechanicals at Theseus's revels.[19]

Their interlude plus masking furthermore reproduces the show characteristic of household winter revels from the early Tudor period onwards, although its performance by such customary visitors is harder to document. Thus the *c.* 1515 household ordinances of the Earl of Northumberland specify for Twelfth Night: 'That their be aithir play as an entirlude A comody or trigidy to be plaied afoir the lord and the laidy afoir the disguising com into the ... Hall.'[20] Interludes and disguisings (in due course elaborated into masques) feature in conjunction at winter revels of the early Tudor monarchs from 1494 onwards,[21] a tradition which continued under Elizabeth. An informative instance is the performance of *Gorboduc* before the Queen in her hall at Westminster on 18 January 1562, followed by 'a great masque': offered as it was by 'the gentlemen of the Temple,' the performance was effectively under customary visit-auspices.[22]

The remaining item, the Presentation, is harder to document, since it is purely subsidiary and therefore unlikely to be mentioned independently. Some may survive in the guise of prologues to interludes or masques, which were often performed, and invariably printed, separately. Uniquely illuminating is Ben Jonson's mock script for an imagined courtesy-visit of London citizens to the royal court, which comprises mainly or only the Presentation. Stripped of satirical colouring and substantial farcical interruptions, 'Christmas his Show' comprises, very much in Quince's manner, a prologue greeting the spectators and announcing the arrival of the performers, the processional entry and circular parade of the latter, to the accompaniment of fife and drum, and the introduction of each of the characters in turn. The performance ends with a dance by these figures which leads straight into Christmas's leave-taking, and must then be the masking ending or constituting the show: some unspecified 'sights' have been lost in between, but we cannot tell if they were to be envisaged as an interlude.[23]

Almost everything in this historical reconstruction – the three-part show of presentation, interlude and masking, performed under the auspices of a seasonal courtesy-visit to a household by dependents from the local community – reappears later in the traditional mummers' plays. While it can no longer be assumed that, as the debris of ancient cult-practices, they necessarily antedate everything and potentially influence anything in medieval and Elizabethan drama, and while we have no evidence of the interludes of recent tradition prior to *c.* 1700, I have argued elsewhere that the overall customs are likely to be survivals of, and so evidence for, precisely the kind of customary activity which Shakespeare reproduces in his Athens revels.[24] For present purposes they usefully suggest that the customary visitors of the financial accounts are very likely to have offered the interlude-plus-masking show which itself is documented from other sources. The mummers' plays may also be appealed to as confirming the traditional status of dramaturgical features of the mechanicals' show, for example the processional entry, the Presenter's introduction of the characters one by one, and the 'contamination' of the interlude by the dramaturgical mode of the Presentation and the masking: the characters in the interludes of mummers' plays are equally given to introducing themselves on their first appearance, using the familiar 'in comes I' formula.

In Shakespeare's play the revels are specifically prompted by a wedding, but the historical evidence suggests that weddings attracted out-of-season appearances of seasonal entertainments, not least those associated with the winter revels. The transfer is explicit in a seventeenth century broadside ballad, 'A merry Wedding Or, O Brave Arthur of Bradley,' describing a wedding to which came 'The chiefest Youths in the Parish ... dancing in a Morrice,' accompanied by girls who performed 'Christmas gambols.'[25] To judge from diarist Henry Machyn's careful observations in the 1550's and 1560's, the masking was the more usual observance at weddings,[26] but both interlude and disguising are specified by the household ordinances of the Earls of Northumberland cited earlier, which laid down that for the wedding supper of an earl's daughter, the bride and groom were to be brought into the great chamber, 'to se suche passe tymes as is their ordurid for theim As disguisinges enterludes or playes.'[27] Actual performance is documented for the wedding in 1526 of the daughter of Sir John Nevill of Chevet, Yorkshire West Riding, celebrated with a banquet, a play and a masque.[28]

Revels on Stage

Discussion of the relationship between *A Midsummer Night's Dream* and household revels has been complicated by the question of whether the play itself was initially written for performance at the wedding revels of an Elizabethan noble household, before being transferred, presumably after suitable adaptation, to the London playhouses,[29] this in turn inordinately confused by the possible court auspices of the wedding and/or the revels, and the presence of the Queen. But with 'Pyramus and Thisbe' as a salutary reminder of how much a play can change in production, the question is not so much the auspices under which *A Midsummer Night's Dream* was first performed, as those under which the play as we have it was performed. And what we have is a first quarto (1600) apparently based on an authorial manuscript, reprinted with little significant change as the second quarto (1619), which in turn was the basis for the text in the 1623 First Folio: this however included 'corrections and additions, mostly stage directions, which appear to derive from the theatre.'[30] The Folio text should evidently be appreciated in terms of playhouse practice, the first quarto in terms of whatever performance auspices Shakespeare had in mind as he was writing it, but there is no external evidence as to what these were, and the first quarto indeed claims on its title page to offer the play *As it hath been sundry times publickely acted, by the Right honourable, the Lord Chamberlaine his seruants.*[31] The reputation of late-Elizabethan printers hardly obliges us to believe this, but more to the point, the few differences between the two versions do not seem to reflect differences in auspices. We lack for this play the correlation of a variant text with alternative (festive) context which Leah S. Marcus explores for *Love's Labour's Lost, King Lear,* and *The Merry Wives of Windsor.*[32]

What follows will therefore reverse the direction of the discussion in favour of the thesis that as a stage-play, which is how we have it, in addition to *depicting* household revels in its penultimate scene, *A Midsummer Night's Dream* in its entirety effectively *recreates* them on stage. Household revels are its *implied* auspices, rather in the way a non-dramatic text can have an implied reader or author.

The implication of revels auspices will be most emphatic during the performance, within the revels its depicts, of an interlude which is riddled with parallels to the host play: the thwarting of young love by domestic circumstances; the night-time flight of the young lovers to a green world where they are subject to the intervention of its denizens, presided over by an emphatically shining moon; the confusions this leads to, accompanied by melodramatic expostulation:

> *Helena.* O weary night! O long and tedious night (3.2.431)
> *Pyramus.* O grim-looked night, O night with hue so black (5.1.167).

The equation will be confirmed almost immediately when it is realized that just as the show of the mechanicals, quite properly for its context, comprises both an interlude and a masking, the same applies, quite remarkably in *its* context, to *A Midsummer Night's Dream*.

Within the show performed by the Lord Chamberlain's Men and published as *A Midsummer Night's Dream* the interlude, as we would expect of a romantic comedy, concludes with the wedding celebrations and anticipations of love's consummation. As always with Shakespeare, the final words are given to the senior figure on stage:

> ... Sweet friends, to bed.
> A fortnight hold we this solemnity
> In nightly revels and new jollity.   *Exeunt.* (5.1.359-61SD)

But if the interlude is over, *A Midsummer Night's Dream* is not, as Puck enters and presents what is effectively a Masque of Fairies, in which, amidst the song and dance of spectacularly guised figures (Oberon, Titania, and 'all their train': 5.1.381SD) characteristic of the masque, comes the expression of benevolence and beneficence to the household (5.1.391) which is at the heart of the genre's social function. Like the Bergamask to which it corresponds, this masque should be given due weight in appreciating the performance as a whole: visual elements will have included Puck sweeping with his broom (5.1.380-81), and the dance-song of the fairies (5.1.384 – 391), enhanced by whatever provides their 'glimmering light,' be it headpieces with lighted candles, or torches.[33] It would add further to the spectacle if the fairies' intention of sprinkling the house with 'field-dew consecrate' (5.1.394ff.) meant that some were carrying flowers, the play having drawn attention to flowers as repositories of dew (2.1.14-15; 4.1.52-55).

In following a play which has effectively ended with a masque, Shakespeare is constructing a dramatic artefact which is distinct from the dramatically integrated disguisings and masques common in interludes and stage-plays from *Fulgens and Lucres* onwards.[34] It would have been a bonus, clearly, if the play as a whole had reproduced the full three-part revels show, with a Presentation as well as an Interlude and Masking, but as Tiffany Stern has observed, prologues were one of those text-segments not necessarily making up the book of the play, and so prone to be missing from the play-as-printed.[35]

What is effectively a Presentation is embedded in the action at the beginning of the play, when the Duke's household is intruded on by visitors from the local community. As a virtual Presenter, entering at the head of a group of four (five, if we follow the quarto text and include Helena), Egeus properly begins with greetings to the householder – 'Happy be Theseus, our renownèd Duke' (1.1.20); declares, like Quince (5.1.109; 112; 113) that he has 'come,' and introduces his three principal characters, his daughter and her two suitors, the latter being explicitly called on, and their roles specified with the 'this man' phrase Quince will use of characters in his company:

> Stand forth Demetrius. – My noble lord,
> This man hath my consent to marry her. –
> Stand forth Lysander. – And, my gracious Duke,
> This hath bewitched the bosom of my child. (1.1.24-27) .

This can be seen as the first item in an implicit wedding-revels show constituted by as much of the romantic plot as is seen by Theseus and his bride. He has himself established the expectation for it by urging his court to 'Stir up the Athenian youth to merriments' (1.1.12), and this Presentation leads on to an interlude constituted by the confrontation between the two suitors, a motif traditional from *Fulgens and Lucres* to the mummers' Wooing Plays. That Theseus sees the performers as those who properly should offer him a customary performance is evident from his reaction the next time he meets them, across his path in the wood on a May morning:

> No doubt they rose up early to observe
> The rite of May, and, hearing our intent,
> Came here in grace of our solemnity (4.1.131-133).

Since 'the rite of May' would almost certainly involve a processional dance by couples (perhaps bearing may-blossom), it is as if Theseus was anticipating their show would end with a Masque of Mayers: the horns which 'wind' to awaken them effectively become part of their performance like the trumpet that heralds Quince and accompanies Pyramus & co.[36]

Nor is this the only revels show built into the play. Puck sees 'Pyramus and Thisbe' in rehearsal (3.1.72ff.), and contrives that in this performance too the interlude is followed by a masking: a figure with an ass's head, plus whatever noise and spectacle are implied from Puck's declaration that he will appear in the form of 'a horse ... a hound, / A hog, a headless bear ...' (3.1.103-4), seen in the light of his earlier declaration that he would be 'An actor, too, perhaps' in the performance (3.1.75). There is a striking antecedent in the celebrated line of dancing, animal-headed masquers depicted in an early fourteenth-century manuscript of the *Romance of Alexander*, who include (alongside ape, goat, bull and griffon) a man wearing an ass's head.[37]

Meanwhile the sequence of woodland scenes of the fairies effectively constitutes a masque, its Presentation the ceremonial entry of the two 'trains' of Oberon and Titania (2.1.59SD), respectively heralded by Puck and a Fairy, the former deploying the conventional call for 'room' (2.1.58) familiar from masques, interludes, and mummers' plays. After the disharmony of the contention about the Indian boy, Titania's train dance 'a roundel and a fairy song' (2.2.1ff.), but the sequence definitively ends with the reconciliation of king and queen, accompanied by music, and symbolized by their taking hands and dancing (4.1.82-85SD).[38]

It is entirely appropriate in this highly metadramatic play with such close – if virtual – affiliations with household revels, that while the various groups in its multiple plot pursue their own trajectories, they are implicitly but demonstrably offering more or less complete customary revels shows (and sometimes for each other), to match and reinforce what the Chamberlain's men were reconstructing for their audience in the playhouse.

Notes

[1] William Shakespeare, *A Midsummer Night's Dream*, ed. Peter Holland, New Oxford Shakespeare / World's Classics (Oxford: Oxford University Press, 1994; repr. 1998). Other Shakespeare texts will be cited from *The Norton Shakespeare*, gen. ed. Stephen Greenblatt (New York: Norton, 1997).

2   For a thorough review of these see David P. Young, *Something of Great Constancy: The Art of 'A Midsummer Night's Dream'* (New Haven: Yale University Press, 1966), pp. 34-48.

3   Tom Pettitt, 'The Living Text: The Play, the Players, and Folk Tradition,' in Sarah Carpenter *et al.* (ed.), *Porci ante Margaritam: Essays in Honour of Meg Twycross* (Leeds: School of English, University of Leeds, 2001), pp. 413-29.

4   Andrew D. Weiner, '"Multiformitie Uniforme": *A Midsummer Night's Dream*,' *ELH*, 38 (1971), pp. 329-349 (p. 345).

5   Edward Berry, *Shakespeare's Comic Rites* (Cambridge: Cambridge University Press, 1984), p. 190; Henry Frank Salerno, 'The Elizabethan Drama and the *Commedia dell' Arte*,' Diss. (University of Illinois, 1956), p. 55.

6   Used to suggest a connection with both the disguising and early forms of the masque. On the complex terminology for this cluster of overlapping traditions see Meg Twycross and Sarah Carpenter, *Masks and Masking in Medieval and Early Tudor England* (Aldershot: Ashgate, 2002).

7   Louis A. Montrose, 'A Kingdom of Shadows,' in D.L. Smith *et al.* (ed.), *The Theatrical City: Culture, Theatre and Politics in London, 1576-1649* (Cambridge: Cambridge University Press, 1955), pp. 68-86 (p. 73).

8   See, respectively, Young, *Something of Great Constancy*, p. 56 (citing Welsford); Holland, *ed. cit.*, p. 93, citing C.L. Barber, *Shakespeare's Festive Comedy* (Princeton: Princeton University Press, 1959).

9   For the most systematic comparison see Clifford Davidson, '"What hempen homespuns have we swagg'ring here?" Amateur Actors in *A Midsummer Night's Dream* and the Coventry Civic Plays and Pageants,' *Shakespeare Studies*, 19 (1987), pp. 87-99.

10 Montrose, 'A Kingdom of Shadows,' p. 70.

11 William Tydeman, *The Theatre in the Middle Ages* (Cambridge: Cambridge University Press, 1978) p. 203.

12 Holland, *ed. cit.*, p. 90; cf. p. 91.

13 On the overall context of household theatre, see Suzanne R. Westfall, *Patrons and Performance: Early Tudor Household Revels* (Oxford: Clarendon Press, 1990).

14 Montrose, pp. 80-81; Penry Williams, 'Shakespeare's *A Midsummer Night's Dream*: Social Tensions Contained,' in *The Theatrical City*, ed. Smith *et al.*, pp. 55-67 (pp. 59-60).

15 *REED: Cumberland, Westmoreland, Gloucestershire*, ed. Audrey Douglas and Peter Greenfield (Toronto: University of Toronto Press, 1986), pp. 347 (text), 395 (translation), 430 (note).

16 F.G. Emmison, *Tudor Food and Pastimes* (London: Benn, 1964), p. 27.

17 David George, 'The Walmesley of Dunkenhalgh Accounts,' *REEDN*, 10.2 (1985), pp. 6-15.

18 Peter H. Greenfield, '"All for your delight / We are not here": Amateur Players and the Nobility,' *RORD*, 28 (1985), pp. 173-180.

19 Williams, 'Shakespeare's *A Midsummer Night's Dream*: Social Tensions Contained,' p. 62.
20 Ian Lancashire, 'Orders for Twelfth Day and Night circa 1515 in the Second Northumberland Household Book,' *English Literary Renaissance*, 10 (1980), pp. 6-45, (p. 34).
21 C.E. McGee and John C. Meagher, 'Preliminary Checklist of Tudor and Stuart Entertainments: 1485-1558,' *RORD*, 25 (1982), pp. 31-114.
22 *The Diary of Henry Machyn*, ed. J.G. Nichols (1848; repr. New York: Johnson Reprint, 1968), p. 275; see also p. 221.
23 *Ben Jonson*, eds. C.H. Herford and P. & E. Simpson, 11 vols., vol. 7 (1941; repr. Oxford: Clarendon Press, 1963), pp. 437-447.
24 '"This man is Pyramus": A Pre-History of the English Mummers' Plays,' *Medieval English Theatre*, 22 (2002 for 2000), pp. 70-99.
25 *The Euing Collection of English Broadside Ballads*, ed. John Holloway (Glasgow: University of Glasgow, 1971), No. 214.
26 *The Diary of Henry Machyn*, Nichols, pp. 82, 215, 248, 288, 300.
27 Lancashire, 'Orders for Twelfth Day and Night,' p. 34n.
28 Ian Lancashire, *Dramatic Texts and Records of Britain: A Chronological Topography to 1558* (Toronto: University of Toronto Press, 1984), p. 111, #537. David Wiles' detailed comparison between 'Pyramus and Thisbe' and English wedding masques in *Shakespeare's Alamanac: A Midsummer Night's Dream, Marriage and the Elizabethan Calendar* (Cambridge: Brewer, 1993), ch. 3, 'The Wedding Masque,' does not take fully into account this duality of the show, and mistakenly claims (p. 47) that 'When Theseus calls for entertainment to pass the three hours between supper and the bedding, he does not expect to be offered a play' (see 5.1.36-37, quoted earlier).
29 On this issue see Harold F. Brooks, ed., *A Midsummer Night's Dream*, Arden Shakespeare (London: Methuen, 1979), Introduction, pp. liii-lvii; Paul N. Siegel, '*A Midsummer Night's Dream* and the Wedding Guests,' *Shakespeare Quarterly*, 4 (1953), pp. 139-144; Wiles, *Shakespeare's Almanac*. The most sustained attempt at refuting revels auspices is Gary Jay Williams, *Our Moonlight Revels: A Midsummer Night's Dream in the Theatre* (Iowa City: University of Iowa Press, 1997), ch. 1, 'The Wedding-Play Myth and the *Dream* in Full Play.'
30 Foakes, ed. NCS, p. 135; see also Brooks, ed., Arden2, p. xxviii.
31 Foakes, p. 135.
32 'Levelling Shakespeare: Local Customs and Local Texts,' *Shakespeare Quarterly*, 42 (1991), pp. 168-78. These circumstances also excuse the present study's use of Peter Holland's Oxford Shakespeare edition, which (see p. 119) while based on Q1, incorporates some 'departures,' including stage directions, from F.
33 See Holland's New Oxford edition notes to 5.1.382; 390-1; 392-413, and (for the torches) Young, *Something of Great Constancy*, p. 22.
34 On the stage tradition see Inga-Stina Ewbank, '"These pretty devices": A Study of Masques in Plays,' in T.J.B. Spenser & S.W. Wells (ed.), *A Book of Masques in*

Honour of Allardyce Nicoll (Cambridge: Cambridge University Press, 1967), pp. 407-48.

[35] Tiffany Stern, *Making Shakespeare: From Stage to Page* (London: Routledge, 2004), pp. 118-119.

[36] This is effectively a generic elaboration on Elliot Krieger's review of these scenes as an interlude effectively staged by Theseus, in '*A Midsummer Night's Dream,*' in *A Midsummer Night's Dream*, New Casebook, ed. Richard Dutton (London: Macmillan, 1996), pp. 38-60 (p. 48).

[37] Oxford, Bodlein Library MS. Bodley 264, fol. 181v, accessible on Early Manuscripts at Oxford University, http://image.ox.ac.uk/.

[38] Young, *Something of Great Constancy*, pp. 57-58 notes the masque-like qualities of each of these moments individually. I have resisted the temptation to identify intervening action (e.g. Titania and Bottom) as an interlude.

SHAKESPEARE'S *TROILUS AND CRESSIDA*: TRAGEDY, COMEDY, SATIRE, HISTORY OR PROBLEM PLAY?

Dorrit Einersen

The question of genre in connection with the story of Troilus and Cressida is complicated. When the story was invented in the 12th century by Benoît de Sainte Maure it formed part of his *Roman de Troie*[1] and was treated as an episode in the story of the fall of Troy.

When Boccaccio[2] took it up c. 1335 he made it a reflection of the narrator's misery at losing his beloved who had left him. He was looking for a story with which to identify, making Troiolo's suffering a mirror of his own. In order to enhance the description of Troiolo's grief he added the story of how he won his beloved, Criseyda, and fulfilled his love for her, although the narrator claims that this is not a reflection of his own experience. So the description of winning and losing love mainly illustrates the common medieval pattern of rising and falling fortune, fortune's wheel. *Il Filostrato* isolates the love story almost completely from the context of the Trojan war, and Troiolo's personal tragedy is followed at the end by a typically medieval antifeminist denunciation of young women who want many lovers and invariably deceive men. 'La donna è mobile' is the conclusion of *Il Filostrato*. The narrator goes on to exhort young men to choose a more mature woman but even so to look out because mature women can also be inconstant. Ironically he ends by entrusting his book to a messenger to carry it to his beloved to make her return to him. It is difficult to imagine that the harsh denunciation of young women would have the desired effect.

Chaucer's poem from c. 1385 was originally named *The Book of Troilus* but later renamed *Troilus and Criseyde*. It opens with a declaration of intent. 'The double sorwe of Troilus to tellen .... My purpos is,' clearly focusing on Troilus and his double sorrow, first in falling in love with Criseyde and thinking that she will never take pity on him, later in losing her when she is exchanged for Antenor and transferred to the Greek camp and after some unspecified time accepts Diomede. The happy fulfilment of their love which fills Book III, and in a circumlocution in the beginning of Book IV is shown to have lasted for 3 years, is not mentioned in the beginning, and the Trojan war is only referred to as part of the medieval pattern of fortune's wheel. As the narrator says fortune sometimes favoured the Greeks and at other times the

Trojans.³ The opening lines of Book IV again stress the importance of fortune. 'But al to litel, weylaway the whyle, / Lasteth swich joie, ythonked be Fortune.' This reversal makes *Troilus and Criseyde* a medieval tragedy, which according to *The Monk's Tale* consists in a man's having experienced prosperity and good fortune and later encountering adversity.⁴ Troilus's happiness is cut off by his losing Criseyde, and in accordance with the courtly love code, which grants a woman sovereignty over her lover, he leaves the decision to her whether to go away with him and so avoid being exchanged with Antenor. Criseyde, who lacks foresight, believes it possible to return to Troilus within 10 days, but as her governing emotion is fear, she gives up her plan and instead finds a new protector and lover, the Greek Diomede. The narrator is divided between pity for her and impatience with her but increasingly focuses on Troilus's pain and suffering. Even when Troilus gets incontrovertible proof that she has been disloyal Troilus says that he cannot unlove her for as much as a quarter of a day.⁵

At the end of the poem Troilus is killed by Achilles and ascends to the eighth sphere, from which he can laugh at the 'blinde lust',⁶ the blind search for pleasure, which leads man astray from loving God and Christ, who will never be false to him. From a Christian perspective Troilus was misguided in his love for a mere weak woman, not a goddess. But the moral is not antifeminist as in the earlier versions of the story. The narrator says

> N'y sey nat this al oonly for thise men
> But moost for wommen that bitraised be
> Thorugh false folk – God yeve hem sorwe, amen! –
> That with hire grete wit and subtilte
> Bytraise yow. And this commeveth me
> To speke, and in effect yow alle I preye,
> Beth war of men, and herkneth whay I seye!⁷

'Men were deceivers ever'. A surprising conclusion to a poem which shows how a woman deceives a man but – as A.C. Spearing says – Criseyde really is betrayed as well as betrayer – betrayed equally by the opportunism of Pandarus and Diomede, and by the idealistic submissiveness of Troilus into a position of 'sovereignty' she cannot sustain. Partly, at least, her infidelity is shown as a consequence of ' The tresoun that to women hath ben do' (II l. 792-793) by society itself. ⁸

Near the end of the poem the narrator ironically calls his poem (which is about 8000 lines long) his 'little tragedy'⁹ and expresses a wish that he will be granted the ability to write a comedy instead. Troilus's suffering opened the poem and filled most of it – in accordance with Andreas Capellanus's opening statement in *The Art of Courtly Love*[10] 'Love is a certain inborn suffering derived from the sight of and excessive meditation upon the beauty of the opposite sex, which causes each one to wish above all things the embraces of the other.' And Troilus's life is so completely dominated by his passion for Criseyde that even after he has won her he only wishes to be with her all the time. When he has lost her he thinks of her every minute. But the comedy the narrator finally wishes he could write may very well be Troilus's ascension to the eighth sphere, which constitutes a divine comedy as well as a Christian consolation.

About a hundred years after Chaucer wrote *Troilus and Criseyde*, Robert Henryson continued the story of Cresseid's fate in *The Testament of Cresseid*. Henryson's narrator is sitting in the cold season writing his sorrowful poem which he calls a tragedy.[11] He claims to be reproducing this from another book than Chaucer's, a book which he claims tells the story of Cresseid's 'fatall destenie.'[12] Henryson's source is probably just as fictive as Chaucer's alleged source, the Latin Lollius. Henryson's poem thus opens as a poem about Cresseid's wretched death. Where Chaucer in Book IV and V focused on Troilus's suffering Henryson's narrator will, he says, report the lamentation and woeful death of the lively Cresseid and tell us about her distress and death. Again we find the medieval pattern of a fall from fortune. Cresseid is repudiated by Diomed, who has fulfilled his lust for her, and – the narrator says – she is reputed to have become a prostitute. In a dream she blames Venus and Cupid for her fading beauty, and the gods in council agree to punish her harshly for her blasphemy. Saturn, the cruellest of the gods, pronounces sentence on her. When she wakes from her dream her beauty is gone and she has been smitten with leprosy, the medieval punishment for loose living. She asks her father, Calchas, who in Henryson's poem is a priest of Venus, to accompany her to a lepers' colony where she complains that she has lost all her good fortune, her life in luxury with beautiful beds, spices and wine, cups of gold and silver and delicious food.[13] In this complaint Cresseid only seems to miss the luxury to which she was accustomed, and it clashes with the narrator's earlier hint that she became a common prostitute. In her complaint Cresseid admonishes every lady of Troy as well as Greece to make a mirror of her and see by her example how good fortune can turn into misfortune. Fortune is fickle, she concludes – as she herself has been.

In Henryson's poem Troilus has not died, but one day he rides by the lepers' colony and on seeing Cresseid is reminded of his former beloved's sweet visage.[14] He even feels a spark of love and passion although neither of the two – the narrator says – recognizes the other. Cresseid is completely changed in appearance, and she has probably lost her eyesight as a result of her leprosy. Troilus throws her a purse full of gold and jewels, and she asks who that was. When she is told that it was the noble and generous Troilus she falls to the ground and repents of her deception saying 'O fals Cresseid and trew knicht Troilus!'[15] She compares her own life in carnal passion and lechery to Troilus's chastity and constancy. She warns men not to trust women who are unstable like weathercocks. She claims that very few women are faithful and ends by blaming only herself for her misfortune. Finally she makes her testament, bequeathing her gold to the lepers. In it she says that she has given Diomed the brooch originally given to her by Troilus. But Troilus's ring is given back to him after her death. He utters the verdict on her 'Scho was untrew and wo is me thairfoir.'[16] The narrator has heard that Troilus erected a tomb with the laconic inscription 'Lo, fair Ladyis, Cresseid of Troyis town, / Sumtime countit the flour of womanheid, / Under this stane, lait lipper, lyis deid.'[17] This stresses the medieval pattern of good fortune, flowering beauty, changed into misfortune, leprosy and suffering. Finally the narrator himself states the intention of his short poem (ballad), which is to admonish worthy women not to mingle their love with false deception.

There is no Christian consolation in Henryson's *Testament of Cresseid*, which is firmly based in a pagan world, but there is a pattern of repentance which is, however, without salvation or grace. Cresseid is not transported into a pagan heaven, nor does she laugh at the end of the poem – as Troilus did in Chaucer.

The reputation of Cresseid had deteriorated after Chaucer, and the common conception of her was that she was a loose woman and a leper.

In Shakespeare's play *Henry V* Pistol calls the prostitute, Doll Tearsheet, a 'lazar kite of Cressid's kind'[18], but another view of her also continues in Shakespeare's time.

In *The Merchant of Venice* Lorenzo says 'In such a night as this ... Troilus, methinks, sighed out his soul toward the Grecian tents where Cressid lay that night'[19] stressing Troilus's love-longing for his lost Cressida but not mentioning that she may have been lying with Diomed.

Shakespeare's play from 1602 is difficult – perhaps impossible – to classify. In the quarto of 1609 it was called 'The Historie of Troylus and Cresseida. As it was acted by the Kings Maiesties seruants at the Globe'. In the second 'state' of the 1609 quarto, the title page reads 'The Famous Historie of Troilus and Cresseid. Excellently expressing the beginning of their loues, with the conceited wooing of Pandarus'. And the publisher's advertisement adds an address to the reader saying 'Eternal reader, you haue here a new play, neuer stal'd with the Stage, neuer clapper-clawd with the palmes of the vulgar, and yet passing full of the palme comicall.' The two quartos thus differ, one claiming that it had been acted at the Globe, the other that it had never appeared on the stage.

Maybe it was performed a couple of times, some think at the Inns of Court rather than at the Globe, where it would have been more appreciated than before a general public, but it was not a popular play. The second quarto claims that it is a comical play. In the Folio edition it is called 'The Tragedie of / Troilus and Cressida'. Placed between the histories and the tragedies in the Folio *Troilus and Cressida* does not fit into either category.

The play opens with a prologue 'In Troy there lies the scene' going on to state what gave rise to the Trojan war, Paris having ravished Helen, Menelaus' queen. The prologue stresses that the play begins in the middle and asks the audience to like it or find fault: 'Now good or bad, 'tis but the chance of war.' The prologue might very well fit a historical play.

Where Boccaccio placed his narrator at the beginning of his poem, Chaucer begins with Troilus's double sorrow, and Henryson's narrator is placed centrally in the poem. In the prologue to Shakespeare's play the focus is on the war as in Benoît, and Troilus is not even mentioned.

When he appears Troilus declares that he will not fight because he has a cruel battle within him and because he is 'weaker than a woman's tear.' Like Boccaccio's and Chaucer's Troilus, Shakespeare's Troilus is struck down by love and effeminate. In a soliloquy he compares Cressida to a pearl of India and himself to a merchant sailing towards her with Pandarus as captain of the ship.[20] Where to Chaucer's Troilus Criseyde was a goddess, far above him, to Shakespeare's Troilus she is a precious pearl that can be won and possessed.

Cressida appears in Act I scene 2. She is witty and quick at repartee like Helen. Pandarus teases her with references to Troilus and says (l. 104) 'I swear to you, I think Helen loves him better than Paris.' Cressida is not shocked but just states 'Then she's a merry Greek indeed,' a woman of loose morals. She appears experienced or a least knowledgeable about sex. In Shakespeare's play she is not a widow as in Boccaccio and Chaucer but a young girl, perhaps only seventeen, as Jan Kott states,[21] without, however, any textual proof. The scene with Pandarus ends in Cressida's flippant declaration 'If I cannot ward what I would not have hit, I can watch you for telling how I took the blow – unless it swell past hiding, and then it's past watching.' (l. 259-261)

In her soliloquy she reveals that she is in love with Troilus but holds off, 'Women are angels, wooing' (l. 277) and she goes on to teach the maxim 'Achievement is command, ungained, beseech' (l. 284). Unlike Chaucer's Criseyde, who is in doubt whether to give up her life as an independent woman, Shakespeare's Cressida seems to regard herself as an object, a thing, which can be won and then despised and perhaps discarded.

In the discussion in the Trojan council in Act II Priam proposes to deliver Helen up and so end the war, and Hector and Troilus quarrel about this. Hector says 'Brother, she is not worth what she doth cost / The holding' (II 2, l. 52-53). Troilus retorts 'What's aught but as 'tis valued?' This can be seen as an idealistic statement, but in Troilus's next long speech he argues that Helen is a pearl (as Cressida is to him) 'whose price has launched above a thousand ships / And turned crowned kings to merchants.'(l. 81-83). Helen's value is not intrinsic but resides in that she has caused so many to fight for her, and later Troilus expressly says that Helen is just 'the theme of honour and renown, / A spur to valiant and magnanimous deeds,'(l. 199-200), a pretext for continuing the war which makes it possible for the Trojans to win glory.

In Act III it appears clearly that the love affair between Troilus and Cressida is not kept secret as it was in Chaucer. Paris hints to Pandarus that Troilus is going to spend the night with Cressida (III 1, l. 83), and Helen flippantly states that if Cressida were to fancy Paris the relationship might have an issue 'Falling in after falling out may make them three' (l. 199), just as Cressida earlier mentioned the possibility that her womb might swell past hiding. To Paris, Helen and Pandarus love means 'hot blood … hot thoughts and hot deeds' as Paris puts it (l. 123-125), love is sexual passion.

This is continued in the next scene where Troilus is waiting for Cressida to appear. Now she is no longer a pearl in India but within reach. But the imagery he uses here is surprising. He mentions the river Styx, the river across which the souls of the dead were to be transported, and wants Pandarus to be his Charon and convey him to the lily-beds in which he may wallow – an ambivalent term but certainly highly sensual (III 2, l. 7-13), Cressida's womb is a lily-bed as in The Song of Songs, but he fears 'swooning destruction' and losing distinction in his joys (l. 21-25). As in a battle he fears destruction and death, the little death of sexual fulfilment or actual death.

The conversation in prose between Pandarus, Troilus and Cressida which follows leaves Troilus bereft of all words and Pandarus poking him to give her deeds instead. Cressida just asks the direct and prosaic question 'Will you walk in, my lord?' (l. 59). Troilus talks about 'the monstruosity in love … that the desire is boundless and the act a slave to limit' (l. 78-80). He promises to be true to Cressida even before their relationship has been consummated (l. 94), thus proclaiming his proverbial status as a paragon of truth.

Now Cressida declares her love for him and even admits that she has kept it secret because she feared he would play the tyrant if she confessed it (l. 118). She is divided between wishing to give in to Troilus and wishing to preserve herself and leave (l. 143-144). Troilus expresses his doubts as to the possibility of a woman's constancy and protests his own truth saying: 'As true as Troilus' (l. 177). Cressida ominously and prophetically says that if she is false she will become a byword for falsehood 'As false as Cressid' (l. 191). The story is familiar so neither Troilus nor Cressida can escape their reputations. Both point to the audience's knowledge of them as emblematic and prophesy what happens later in the play. Pandarus enters into the role-playing game saying 'let all pitiful goers-between be called to the world's end … panders' (l. 195-199). In Chaucer likewise Pandarus at one point wonders whether he can be called a bawd for bringing Troilus and Criseyde together but comforts himself by saying that he has done everything out of friendship for Troilus and not for money.

Pandarus then shows Troilus and Cressida to a chamber with a bed and exhorts them to 'press it to death' (l. 4).

This scene is immediately followed by Calchas's wish to buy his daughter from the Trojans in exchange for Cressida. Diomed is sent to fetch her.

In Act IV scene 2 Cressida and Troilus rise from their one night together, and Cressida says 'Are you aweary of me?' (l. 8) as she had feared in the beginning of the play. She goes on 'Prithee tarry. You men will never tarry. / O foolish Cressid, I might have still held off, / And then you would have tarried' (l. 17-19). Just as Troilus kept harping on his own truth and fear that a woman cannot be true Cressida has her preconceptions of men. They soon lose interest in a woman after having won her.

Aeneas and Diomed then enter. They know they will find Troilus and Cressida together and have come to fetch her. Troilus can only ask 'Is it concluded so?' (l. 68), he cannot or at least does not protest, but he goes on 'How my achievements mock me!' (l. 71) thinking more of his own conquering and winning his pearl, his prey, than of Cressida's feelings. Pandarus likewise shows no sympathy for Cressida but exclaims 'Would thou hadst ne'er been born! I knew thou wouldst be his death' (l. 86-87) showing that he is only Troilus's friend. Cressida – it seems – is to be blamed for her father's wish to have her back. Only Cressida herself protests saying 'O you immortal gods! I will not go' (l. 95), but even she is tainted with antifeminist prejudices or aware of her prescribed role when she exclaims

'Make Cressid's name the very crown of falsehood / If ever she leave Troilus!' (l. 100-101) although it is hard to blame her for being treated as an object and a pawn in the tactical game of the men. She gives vent to her grief immoderately whereas Troilus blames 'injurious Time' for scanting them with a single famished kiss (l. 46). Grief at parting makes Cressida emotional but Troilus philosophical. But soon after Cressida prophetically says 'A woeful Cressid 'mongst the merry Greeks!' (l. 55) and seems to foresee that the merry, licentious Greeks may console her for her loss of Troilus.

Unlike Chaucer's Troilus, Shakespeare's Troilus promises to corrupt the Grecian sentinels to visit her nightly. But his fears now turn into jealousy. The Greeks can sing, dance, speak sweetly and play at subtle games where he himself is just simple and true.

Diomed starts wooing Cressida at once in the presence of Troilus and states 'When I am hence, / I'll answer to my lust' (4.4., l. 130-131) – a deliberately ambivalent phrase meaning either 'I'll do what I please' or 'I'll fulfil my lust.' He goes on to say 'To her own worth / She shall be prized' (l. 132-133). He will not overvalue her. To him she is not a precious pearl but an available woman he feels certain he can conquer and possess.

The most dramatic scene in the play is Act IV scene 5 where Diomed enters the Greek camp with Cressida. First Agamemnon kisses her welcome, and Ulysses suggests that they should all kiss her. At first she passively receives their kisses but gradually she uses her wit and talent for quick repartee as she did in the beginning of the play. Ulysses, who suggested the kissing-game, refuses to kiss her before Helen becomes a maid again which is never.

Depending on the way this scene is acted Cressida can appear frightened and forced to take part in the men's game or on top of the situation, playing with the men. Ulysses sums her up as a sensual, wanton woman, a slut, a daughter of the game i.e. a prostitute (l. 55-63). Here she becomes a parallel to Henryson's Cresseid and a clear contrast to Troilus, whom Ulysses calls a true knight ... matchless firm of word' (l. 97—98) but – he adds – he can also be vindictive.

Troilus keeps his word, enters the Greek camp and asks Ulysses to convey him to Calchas' tent where Ulysses tells him Diomed is wooing Cressida. So Troilus is prepared for the transference of her love. Love is generally – he says – 'food for Fortune's tooth' (l. 293).

Outside Calchas's tent Diomed and Cressida play a game where she is partly reluctant and partly willing to give in. The scene is witnessed by Ulysses, Troilus and Thersites, the bitter and cynical commentator. He sums up the situation 'How the devil Luxury, with his fat rump and potato finger, tickles these together!' (l. 57-58). Diomed demands of Cressida the sleeve that Troilus had given her as a token of love and a pledge. When she gives in she is aware that her new lover will not love her the way Troilus did. She realizes that she will be plagued (l. lll) an ambivalent phrase meaning plagued by bad conscience, suffering or perhaps smitten with the plague, a veiled reference to Henryson's Cresseid, who was smitten with leprosy.

She bids Troilus farewell saying 'One eye yet looks on thee / But with my heart the other eye doth see. / Ah, poor our sex! This fault in us I find / The error of our eye directs our mind' (l. 113-116). Not only she but all women, she implies, are swayed by their eyes and self-divided. In Guido delle Colonne's translation of Benoît this was phrased as follows 'if one of their eyes weeps (for leaving her lover) the other smiles out of the corner (to invite another lover).'[22] These are the last words Cressida utters in the play condemning herself and all women, and they are followed by Thersites' aside 'A proof of strength she could not publish more, / Unless she said, "My mind is now turned whore"'(l. 119-120), hinting at her future fate as a parallel to Henryson's Cresseid.

Troilus's reaction is at first to try to deny what he has seen, then to condemn all women including his own mother. If Cressida can deceive him she taints all women. Just as Hamlet thought that his mother's granting his uncle her favour tainted the whole female sex including Ophelia, so Troilus pronounces all women guilty. But his final solution is to divide Cressida into two, Diomed's Cressida and his own beloved. Chaos reigns and 'the fragments, scraps, the bits and greasy relics / Of her o'ereaten faith, are bound to Diomed' (l. 155-167). Where he anticipated tasting 'Love's thrice-repured nectar' (3.2, l. 20) in his encounter with Cressida what she can give Diomed is only greasy, unappetizing relics. His love for Cressid is transformed into hatred of Diomed and a wish for revenge, a wish that is not granted. Troilus lives on, and Pandarus ends the play bequeathing his venereal diseases to the audience.

The only tragic death is that of Hector but not even that is truly tragic: he covets the armour of a dead Greek warrior, and when he has unarmed to put it on he is attacked and killed by Achilles' Myrmidons, who take advantage of his vulnerability. Hector's death is reported briefly and laconically by Troilus with the following words 'Hector is dead. There is no more to say' (l. 22). Nobody utters any words of praise for 'the noblest Trojan of them all.'

The play as a whole leaves an impression of futility. The war goes on and on although it could easily have ended if the Trojans had given up Helen, who in the play is just a superficial coquette. But that would make all the lives which have been lost meaningless and it still provides a pretence to win glory.

Jan Kott says 'In tragedy the protagonists die, but the moral order is preserved …. In this amazing play Troilus neither dies himself, nor does he kill the unfaithful Cressida. There is no catharsis.'[23]

Oscar J. Campbell has called *Troilus and Cressida* a comical satire. According to Campbell Shakespeare satirized not only Cressida but Troilus, not only Greeks but Trojans. There are elements of a comical satire in the play especially in the figure of Thersites, who in Act II scene 3 sums up the war as follows 'all the argument is a whore and a cuckold; a good quarrel to draw emulous factions and bleed to death upon. Now the dry serpigo on the subject, and war and lechery confound all!'[24] But the comedy is bitter and dark, and the ending of the play with Pandarus's bequeathing his diseases to the audience unpleasant and grotesque.

Troilus and Cressida has also been called a problem play because of its moral ambivalence. In his introduction to *Shakespeare's Problem Plays* E.M.W. Tillyard remarks 'Many readers have found in the Problem Plays a spirit of gloom, disillusion and morbidity that exceeds dramatic propriety.'[25] He stresses the ambivalence of the matter of Troy to the Elizabethans: 'The Trojan War was both romantic and fought for an unworthy cause. Some of the fighters were true knights but committed moral errors, some were ignoble. Troilus was both a comic and a grim figure. Cressida was a faithless woman, but the course of her infidelity and the state of mind dictating it could vary very widely.'[26] In Chaucer's *Troilus and Criseyde* the narrator tried to excuse and empathize with Criseyde, in Henryson Cresseid was turned into a loose woman and was punished with leprosy, and although she repents there is no saving grace in the poem. Shakespeare's Cressida only incidentally recalls Henryson's, rather she is in Jan Kott's characterization 'would-be cynical … afraid of feelings. She distrusts herself. She is our contemporary because of this self-distrust, reserve, and need of self-analysis. She defends herself by irony.'[27]

Jan Kott calls *Troilus and Cressida* 'amazing and modern.' What makes it modern is its multiple perspectives and points of view. Troilus can be seen as an idealist or a sensualist, as effeminate or as a great warrior, second only to Hector. Cressida can be seen as a precious pearl (as Troilus sees her in the beginning) or as a wanton and a whore (as Ulysses and Thersites see her). Through Polonius in *Hamlet* Shakespeare satirizes the tendency to label plays as 'tragedy, comedy, history, pastoral, pastoral-comical, historical-pastoral, tragical-historical, tragical-comical-historical-pastoral.'[28] Shakespeare's plays are often difficult to categorize, the comedies frequently have tragical elements in them and the tragedies contain scenes of pure comedy. So *Troilus and Cressida* can perhaps be called a historical-tragical-comical-satirical problem play.

Notes

[1] Benoît de Sainte Maure, *Le Roman de Troie* ed. L. Constans (Paris 1904-12).
[2] *Chaucer's Boccaccio, ed.* and *trans.* by N.R. Havely (Cambridge: D.S. Brewer 1980).
[3] Geoffrey Chaucer, *Troilus and Criseyde*, in *The Riverside Chaucer*, ed. Larry D. Benson (New York: Oxford University Press 1987) ll. 134-140.
[4] The Monk's Tale, l. 1991-1996.
[5] Chaucer, V, l. 1698.
[6] Chaucer, V, l. 1824.
[7] Chaucer, V, l. 1779-1785.
[8] A.C. Spearing, *Troilus and Criseyde* (London: Edward Arnold 1976) p. 53.
[9] Chaucer, V, l. 1786.
[10] *The Art of Courtly Love* trans. from Latin *De arte honeste amandi* by John Jay Parry (New York: Unger, 1970 (1941)
[11] Robert Henryson, *The Testament of Cresseid*, ed. Denton Fox (London: Nelson, 1968), l. 4.
[12] Henryson, l. 62.
[13] Henryson, ll. 417-420.
[14] Henryson ll. 498-504.
[15] Henryson, l. 553.
[16] Henryson, l. 602.
[17] Henryson, ll. 607-609.
[18] *Henry V* 2.1.76.
[19] *The Merchant of Venice* V 1, 1-5.
[20] William Shakespeare, *Troilus and Cressida* ed. David Bevington (Walton-on-Thames: Nelson, 1998), I, 1, 91-100. Subsequent references to this text are given in parenthesis in the article.
[21] Jan Kott, *Shakespeare Our Contemporary* (London: Methuen, 1964), p. 66.
[22] Guido delle Colonne, *Historia destructionis Troiae* 1287, tr. Mary Elizabeth Meek (Bloomington IN: Indiana University Press 1974). Quoted from Robert P. Miller (ed.), *Chaucer: Sources and Backgrounds* (New York: Oxford University Press, 1977) p. 311.
[23] Jan Kott, p. 68.
[24] Oscar James Campbell, *Comical Satyre and Shakespeare's 'Troilus and Cressida'* (San Marino, California, 1938), pp. 69-72.
[25] E.M.W. Tillyard, *Shakespeare's Problem Plays* (Middlesex, England, Peregrine Books 1965 (1950)), p. 10.
[26] Tillyard, p. 50.
[27] Jan Kott, p. 66.
[28] William Shakespeare, *Hamlet*, Act II, scene 2, ll. 392-395.

TROILUS AND CRESSIDA:
A DIALOGIC READING

Michael Skovmand

The immediate historical context of a play-text is its performance history. One incontrovertible fact about about *Troilus and Cressida* should be mentioned at the outset: there is no *record* of any Elizabethan or Jacobean performance of the play. *Troilus and Cressida* is very much a 20th century play in terms of its performance history. Consequently, any consideration of the early performance history or audience relations of the play is bound to be conjectural. However, as Annabel Patterson has pointed out, the dramatic function as defined by Shakespeare, with Hamlet as a mouthpiece, '... to show virtue her feature, scorn her own image, and the very age and body of the time his form and pressure' (*Hamlet*, III, 2, 22-24) points to a generally *mimetic* dimension of the plays, which, according to Patterson, indicates how Shakespeare, particularly, I would suggest, in this middle phase of his career, was concerned 'to allow the pressure of contemporary events and issues to imprint itself on his plays.'[1] The following reading of the Prologue and the first three acts of the play will be a continuous process of 'squinting' between what may be called the *diegetic* and the *mimetic* dimensions of the play – Plato's original distinction between the speech of the poet, and the imitation of speech of characters, from Book III of *The Republic*.

Any reading which is concerned with the genre of a text is bound to commute between diegetic and mimetic aspects, in the sense that the operation is a process of squinting, between the concrete text at hand and more general notions of similar or different classes of texts or modes of expression. What is remarkable, however, about *Troilus and Cressida* is the way in which the text is not only in dialogue with its historical and generic context, that is to say, in relation to previous and contemporary notions about the cumulative range of stories about the fall of Troy, and about traditional and contemporary notions about definitions of tragedy, comedy, history and satire, but concurrently, the play itself, in its diegetic dimension, is, quite simply, in a continuous dialogue with itself.

What does this mean, and what are the implications of this for a reading of the play? There is in *Troilus and Cressida* no consistent authorial focus of sympathy; no group, character, position or action which is unambiguously identified as good, positive, approved of by the author. There seems to be, in other words, no invitation on the part of the author to empathy or identification.

A. The Prologue:

One obvious point to be made about the Prologue in *Troilus and Cressida* is the fact that it is there at all. Before the writing of *Troilus and Cressida* Shakespeare had only used a Prologue twice, and in both cases as choric functions: in *Romeo and Juliet* and in *Henry V*, and he was to do it only once after *Troilus and Cressida*, in *Henry VIII*. In other words, Shakespeare's use of a Prologue is not a reflection of his own habitual dramatic practice. His use of it in *Romeo and Juliet* (c.1595) reflects his awareness of using well-known material, as well as his desire to provide a traditional choric perspective on the action. His use of Prologue/Chorus in *Henry V* (c.1599) is quite extraordinary for his history plays, providing an ongoing commentary, and metacommentary, continuously appealing to the imaginative faculties of the audience: 'Think when we talk of horses that you see them...' (Prol. l. 26). This contributes to the declamatory, at times celebratory quality of *Henry V*, setting it apart from the other history plays of Shakespeare. Continuous audience address invites distance, and discourages empathy and identification. The Prologue in *Troilus and Cressida*, I suggest, although it does not continue as a choric character in the play, has a similar function. Had Shakespeare wanted historical *Einfühlung* along the lines of *Anthony and Cleopatra* or *Julius Caesar*, the prologue would have been counterproductive. Shakespeare wanted a means of distantiation to set the tone, and establish the right genre contract with the audience, and a slightly *kitsch* Prologue, complete with intertextual allusions, would do the job.

The Prologue was not included in the 1609 Quarto, but appeared, with a different typeface than the rest of the text, in the First Folio. It is hardly possible to imagine it being written especially for the 1623 Folio – there is nothing about it to suggest that it is not from Shakespeare's hand. Indeed the reference to 'A Prologue arm'd, but not in confidence' (l. 23) must be a direct reference to the Prologue in Ben Jonson's *Poetaster* from 1601:

> If any muse why I salute the stage,
> An armed *Prologue*; know 'tis a dangerous age:
> Wherein, who writes, had need present his *Scenes*
> Fortie-fold proofe against the conjuring meanes
> Of base detractors and illiterate apes,
> That fill up roomes in fair and formall shapes.
> 'Gainst these, have we put on this forc't defence:
> Whereof the *allegorie* and hid sence
> Is, that a well erected confidence
> Can fright their pride, and laugh their folly hence.

Compare this passage to Shakespeare's equivalent one in *Troilus and Cressida*, and the correspondence between the two is apparent:

> –   And hither am I come,
> A Prologue arm'd, but not in confidence
> Of author's pen or actor's voice, but suited
> In like conditions as our argument,
> To tell you, fair beholders, that our play
> Leaps o'er the vaunt and firstlings of those broils,
> Beginning in the middle, starting thence away
> To what may be digested in a play.
> Like or find fault: do as your pleasures are:
> Now good or bad, 'tis but the chance of war.   (Prologue, ll. 22-31)

The combination of the armed prologue and the theme of authorial confidence both in Jonson and Shakespeare is ample evidence that Shakespeare is unambiguously referring to Jonson's Prologue, thus giving the dating of *Troilus and Cressida* a firm *terminus a quo*, i.e. 1601. Jonson has his Prologue wear arms, because of the attacks he suffers from 'base detractors and illiterate apes' – presumably the likes of Marston, Shakespeare and Dekker in the so-called 'War of the Theatres', or 'Poetomachia'. Shakespeare, in his reply, argues that *his* Prologue is not wearing the armour in confidence of the author's pen or the actor's voice, but is dressed in a warlike way, as befits the subject matter. Shakespeare carries on the polemics, implicitly, by his final couplet, addressed to the audience:

> Like or find fault: do as your pleasures are
> Now good or bad, 'tis but the chance of war.

This is a comment on Jonson's 'swear[ing] that his play were good' from the *Poetaster* Prologue, following naturally from the previous reference. But what is the issue that Shakespeare is referring to? I submit that this particular exchange in the 'War of the Theatres' is a very precise indication of Shakespeare's authorial position. Unlike Jonson, whose satirical plays of this period, not only *Poetaster*, but also *Every Man out of his Humour* and *Cynthia's Revels*, are intensely personal, with continuous confrontations with and innuendo towards rival authors, Shakespeare's interest is in the subject matter – his 'argument' as he puts it.[2] *Troilus and Cressida*, unlike Jonson's polemical plays, is not a '*roman à clef*', to be searched for allusions to contemporary personages. The polemic of *Troilus and Cressida* is of a more general nature. Its object is the contemporary status of the subject 'The Fall of Troy' as basis for drama, and by extension, the nature of heroic drama in general. A number of features in the Prologue contribute towards this generic understanding of the play, towards the early establishment of a genre contract with the audience which attempts to strike a balance between local polemical satire directed at contemporary treatments of the Troy theme: notably Chapman's translation of parts of *The Iliad* in 1598 and possibly one or two plays by Dekker and Chettle from 1599 (of which only a fragment of a 'Plot' exists),[3] and on the other hand, Shakespeare's high-spirited and at times mischievous exploration of the overlapping areas of comedy, tragedy, history and satire. Shakespeare, of course, had already demonstrated his knowledge of the Troy story several times in his works prior to *Troilus and Cressida*. There are numerous brief references to this material in the plays of Shakespeare preceding the composition of *Troilus and Cressida*[4] which suggest that the Troy story, in all its ramifications and historical transmutations, was an established part of Shakespeare's mental library, as must have been the case with all of his educated contemporaries.

B: *Troilus and Cressida*: **the play-text.**
Shakespeare's opening scenes, more often than not, are like stem cells, out of which the whole universe of the play can be constructed. With a Prologue to strike the initial chords, organising initial audience expectations, the first scene of Act one establishes the audience contract with the *diegesis*, i.e the world of the play. The opening lines are quite to the point:

                    Enter Pandarus and Troilus.
Troil.   Call here my varlet, I'll unarm again,
            Why should I war without the walls of Troy,
            That find such cruel battle here within?
            Each Trojan that is master of his heart
            Let him to field: Troilus, alas, hath none.
Pand.   Will this gear ne'er be mended?
Troil.   The Greeks are strong, and skilful to their strength,
            Fierce to their skill and to their fierceness valiant;
            But I am weaker than a woman's tear,
            Tamer than sleep, fonder than ignorance,
            Less valiant than the virgin in the night,
            And skilless as unpractis'd infancy.
Pand.   Well, I have told you enough of this: for my part I'll not meddle nor
            make no farther. He that will have a cake out of the wheat must
            tarry the grinding.

A basic counterpoint is set up between two opposed discourses, that of Troilus and Pandarus, between the young prince and Cressida's uncle, between the inflated rhetoric of Troilus's blank verse and the homespun kitchen metaphors of Pandarus' prose. The very first line of this supposedly heroic play, paradoxically, is about Troilus wanting to *unarm*, because of the 'cruel battle within' – his lovesickness for Cressida, in which matter he is urging Pandarus to be his go-between. With a few deft strokes, Shakespeare has broached the major themes of the play: Love and War, and through the instant deflation of Troilus' rhetorical inflation, the genre: that of humorous satire. The rest of this expository scene reiterates this counterpoint of inflation and deflation, in the exchange between the discourses of Troilus and Pandarus.

However, unlike plays such as *Romeo and Juliet*, *Hamlet* or *Antony and Cleopatra*, this is not an expository scene performed by peripheral characters. Troilus and Pandarus may have been marginal to Homer, but to Shakespeare they are major characters throughout the play. Shakespeare, accordingly, demonstrates from the very first his fundamental dramatic choices: the prologue told us that we would be starting *in medias res* of the siege of Troy; now we learn that two peripheral Homeric characters will take centre stage, and that the main optics of the play will be through the story of Troilus's longings for Cressida – a non-Homeric character identified with unfaithfulness since Chaucer's poem *Troilus and Criseyde*.

The following scene – Cressida watching the Trojan princes return from war – again thwarts our expectations. It has an obvious expository function – introducing us to Cressida, the quickwitted, bawdy wench, in the company of her servant and her uncle Pandarus, the latter intent on 'selling' Troilus to her. Again, a counterpoint is organised between two opposed discourses, this time not between the inflated rhetoric of Troilus and the down-to-earthness of Pandarus, but, on the contrary, with Pandarus in the 'naive' role of the over-anxious salesman, and Cressida performing the deflating, with her quick wit and bawdy cynicism. At the end of the scene, with Cressida alone on stage, Shakespeare offers the audience an inside view of Cressida, through what is not so much a soliloquy as an aside-like speech to the audience, in which she reveals her true feelings for Troilus, along with her strategy of playing hard to get:

> Words, vows, gifts, tears, and love's full sacrifice
> He offers in another's enterprise
> But more in Troilus thousand-fold I see
> Than in the glass of Pandar's praise may be;
> Yet hold I off. Women are angels, wooing:

> Things won are done; joy's soul lies in the doing.
> That she belov'd knows naught that knows not this:
> Men prize the thing ungain'd more than it is. (I, 1, 286-293)

This is a far cry from Juliet's admission:

> ... I am too fond
> And therefore thou mayest think my behaviour light,
> But trust me, gentleman, I'll prove more true,
> Than those that have more coying to be strange. (*Romeo and Juliet*, II, 2, 98-101)

There is a world of hard-won experience behind Cressida's philosophy, so obviously at odds with Troilus's self-deceiving, inflated view of her: 'her hand, in whose comparison all whites are ink,' (I, 1, 55-56), and 'Her bed is India; there she lies, a pearl.' (I, 1, 100). By the end of Act I, scene 2, the audience no longer harbours any illusions about the heroic nature of this play. The Trojans, traditionally heroic favourites with the English against the more mercenary Greeks, are here presented from the oblique angles of a Pandarus, a Cressida, and an infatuated Troilus, in all their ordinariness.

Next follows, as a striking contrast, an expository scene from the Greek camp. It is a council of war, dominated by the speeches of Agamemnon, Nestor and Ulysses, with Ulysses as the obvious chief strategist. The contrast between Cressida's matter-of factness and Agamemnon's convoluted, tortuous discourse could hardly be greater:

> The ample proposition that hope makes
> In all designs begun on earth below
> Fails in the promis'd largeness: checks and disasters
> grow in the veins of actions highest rear'd,
> As knots, by the conflux of meeting sap,
> Infects the sound pine and diverts his grain
> Tortive and errant from his course of growth... (I, 3, 3-9)

Making the lame point that things don't always turn out the way we hope in this roundabout way, Agamemnon is indirectly characterized as a puffed-up, long-winded fool. This is furthermore borne out by two additional circumstances: the fact that Aeneas, emissary from the Trojan camp, does not recognize Agamemnon, whether deliberately or not, and the fact that Agamemnon is effectively left out of the strategy talk between Ulysses and Nestor, in which Ulysses broaches his plan to deliberately bypass Achilles and select Ajax instead for the duel with Hector. Nestor is reduced to being an echo of both Agamemnon and Ulysses, and made out to be the rather ridiculous *senex iratus*, who is prepared to take on Hector if no one else will. Ulysses, accordingly, appears to be the first *authorized* character we meet in the play, i.e. the first character whose speech or action is not undercut or satirized by the speech or action of any other character. In this slippery world of multiple ironies, he seems unchallenged by competing discourses. Does that mean, then, that his great speech on 'degree' should be taken at face value? I think not. It is not, as Kenneth Palmer puts it, 'a text to which the play is a sermon'.[5] The Ulysses speech is perhaps the text whose 'authority' is the most contested among all the major character statements in Shakespeare's works:

> O, when degree is shak'd
> Which is the ladder of all high designs,
> The enterprise is sick....
> Then everything includes itself in power,
> Power into will, will into appetite,
> And appetite, an universal wolf,
> So doubly seconded with will and power,
> Must make perforce an universal prey,
> And last eat up himself. (I, 3, 99-124)

Ulysses may be 'authorized' as far as his analysis of the situation is concerned, *in abstracto*, that is. The actual delivery of this speech, including the dramatic situation in which it is made, does not in itself undercut the validity of its indictment of the present state of affairs. There is nothing to suggest that Shakespeare does not sympathise, or even identify with the concern about social and moral disruption expressed in the speeches. But the plays are not moral treatises, they are dramas. And Shakespeare's interests as a dramatist are not with abstract principles as such, but with the conflicts generated when abstract principles collide with living human beings. As Agamemnon, in one of his rare moments of insight, puts it, in response to Ulysses' speech: 'The nature of the sickness found, Ulysses, / What is the remedy?' (I, 3, 140-41).[6]

The remedy, however, is not suggested right away. Instead, we get further instancing of the 'sickness', more specifically of Achilles, who 'in his tent/ lies mocking our designs' with Patroclus, his 'male harlot'. Ulysses, in graphic detail, tells the Greek leaders how Achilles makes Patroclus parody them, in particular Agamemnon and Nestor, implicitly parodying them *himself*.

This is one of several scenes in *Troilus and Cressida* which illustrate the dialogical principle at work in the play. Ulysses, in identifying the 'sickness', i.e. the mental paralysis of the Greek camp, mimics the mimicry of Patroclus and Achilles, and in so doing indirectly undercuts the authority of the Greek leaders, in order to strengthen his own position. Indeed the play becomes a Chinese box system, or perhaps rather a hall of mirrors, in which Shakespeare 'mimics' the Troy story in which Ulysses mimics Agamemnon and Patroclus's mimicry of the Greek leaders. Actually, there is an additional 'meta-level' of mimicry, in that Ulysses refers to Patroclus's *style* of acting, probably simultaneously mimicking it:

>...Sometimes, great Agamemnon,
> Thy topless deputation he puts on,
> And *like a strutting player*, whose conceit
> Lies in his hamstring and doth think it rich
> To hear the wooden dialogue and sound
> 'Twixt his stretch'd footing and the scaffoldage,
> Such to-be-pitied and o'erwrested seeming
> He acts thy greatness in. (I, 3,151-158: my italics)

As pointed out by Armstrong and others,[7] the 'strutting player', so well known from Hamlet's speech to the players and Macbeth's final soliloquy, refers to a convention of stylized declamatory acting, of which Shakespeare seems particularly critical. So the *contemporary extradiegetic* mimicry of both the Troy story and acting conventions coexist with the *intradiegetic* representation of Ulysses mimicking Achilles and Patrocles's mimicry for his own strategic purposes. Ulysses's point is that that this mimicry is demeaning and demoralising. All the achievements of the Greek camp 'serves/ as stuff for these two to make paradoxes', as he puts it. Nestor immediately jumps on the wagon, criticising Ajax and Thersites for their criticisms of the Greek war effort, which they call 'bed-work, mapp'ry, closet-war'. The interesting point, of course, is that the critics have a real point. The 'phony war' of attrition, the seven years' siege of Troy, runs counter to the conventions of heroic warfare, undermining as it does the instinctive urge for confrontation and combat, and in the process undermining 'degree', specifically the hierarchy of command.

Ulysses is the mastermind behind this strategy of attrition. He is also capable of thinking on his feet, as he responds to the Trojan countermove: a one-on-one confrontation between Hector and the top Greek Warrior – presumably Achilles. Agamemnon is taken in by Aeneas, whereas Ulysses has 'a young conception in [his] brain' – which is to choose Ajax instead of Achilles, thereby achieving two things simultaneously: avoiding the risk of losing Achilles, and enraging Achilles sufficiently to make him fit for later action – a sophisticated ploy of reverse psychology, and a win-win situation for the Greeks.

The corresponding 'big scene' in the Trojan camp, of stocktaking and soul-searching, does not follow immediately as Act II opens. Instead we are introduced to two characters referred to, and negatively, in the previous scene, Ajax and Thersites, subsequently joined by another male couple, Achilles and Patroclus. The scene, ostensibly about the proclamation of a duel with an as yet unspecified opponent, is among the nastiest in Shakespeare's collected works, a continuous series of insults, invective and physical abuse, giving ample and concrete evidence of the state of affairs discussed in more general terms in the previous scene. The next scene (Act II, scene 2), i.e. the 'big' Trojan council of war, contrasts mightily by its civilized, measured rhetoric. And yet the subject of discussion is the most important of all: whether to give up Helen, and in so doing satisfy the Greek camp and have the siege raised. Shockingly, Hector, supreme hero of the Trojan camp, coolly suggests: 'Let Helen go.' – 'She is not worth what she doth cost the keeping' (II, 2, 17/ 52)! The ensuing discussion is between Troilus and Hector, and is as central to the play as Ulysses's 'degree' speech. It is about the objective and subjective nature of value:

> *Hect.*   Brother,
>   She is not worth what she doth cost the keeping.
> *Troil.*   What's aught but as 'tis valued?
> *Hect.*   But value dwells not in particular will:
>   It holds his estimate and dignity
>   As well wherein 'tis precious of itself
>   As in the prizer. 'Tis mad idolatry
>   To make the service greater than the god;
>   And the will dotes that is attributive
>   To what infectiously itself affects,
>   Without some image of th'affected merit.
> *Troil.*   ...There can be no evasion
>   To blench from this and to stand firm by honour. (II, 2, 51-61/68-73)

After Paris's obvious argument as Helen's husband, and Cassandra's rhapsodic prophecy about the burning of Troy, Hector strangely sums up the argument, saying that morally it was wrong to abduct Helen, and worse to keep her; nevertheless, he agrees with Troilus that they should keep her:

>   For 'tis a cause that hath no mean dependence
>   Upon our joint and several dignities.
> Troil.   Why, there you touch'd the life of our design:
>   Were it not glory that we more affected
>   Than the performance of our heaving spleens,
>   I would not wish a drop of Trojan blood
>   Spent more in her defence. But, worthy Hector,
>   She is a theme of honour and renown,
>   A spur to valiant and magnanimous deeds,
>   Whose present courage may beat down our foes,
>   And fame in time to come canonize us; (II, 3, 193-203)

Many attempts have been made to make sense of Hector's amazing *volte-face* in this debate. What I propose is a reading which focuses on the obvious point of this dramatized dispute over value: the spurious nature of the argument, and the volatility of the character positions. Shakespeare, it seems to me, was concerned to expose the extraordinary *folly* of the Trojan War. The two 'big' scenes in the Greek and Trojan camps testify precisely to that – to the glaring contradictions between the rhetoric and real lived relations in the two camps.

Troilus may win the present argument with Hector. He is, of course, oblivious to the fact that he himself will be very personally embroiled in the problematic of giving up a woman to the enemy – Cressida.

This scene, in other words, like its Greek counterpart in Act I, 3, is riddled with dramatic ironies and paradoxes, to such an extent that by this point in the play dramatic ironies and paradoxes have acquired the prominence of an organising principle for the drama as a whole, as a set of optics or generic system. The system, to use the Bakhtinian term, is *dialogical*. It involves two basic principles of organisation: the notion of a multiplicity (or at least two) of actively competing voices, and the renunciation of positive authorization. It is this *double de-centering* which is the organising principle of *Troilus and Cressida*.The following long scene, Act II, scene 3, externalizes this dialogical principle. It is a scene of the kind that we would normally associate with opera: several simultaneous voices taking turns, with single lines, either with repartees or asides, stretching the illusion of selective hearing on stage to the bursting point. Ajax is manipulated into assuming Achilles' part in the duel against Hector, and in the process exposed as the slow-witted fool he is.

Act III opens with quickwitted dialogue between secondary characters, in this case Pandarus and Paris's servant, as a warm-up for the introduction of Helen of Troy, the apple of discord of the Trojan War. Again, Shakespeare thwarts expectations and gives us a Helen who seems to vindicate Hector's argument in the previous act that 'she is not worth what she doth cost the keeping' – frivolous, bawdy, and none too bright. Indeed the so-called 'love song' that Paris and Helen ask Pandarus to sing (III, 1, 110-121), is nothing but a bawdy ditty exploiting the conventional Renaissance trope of conflating death and sexual orgasm, indeed mimicking the sounds of sexual intercourse.

Then follows the major love scene between Troilus and Cressida, one of the strangest of its kind in Shakespeare's plays. Again, indeed from the outset, the theme of sexual gratification is linked with that of death. Troilus' hyperbolical rhetoric is strangely inappropriate to the occasion, comparing himself as he does to a soul preparing for the passage to Hades.

Troilus is entirely self-absorbed, ruminating upon how he will react to the sensory experience of being with Cressida, fearing to 'lose distinction in my joys/ As doth a battle, when they charge on heaps/The enemy flying.' (III, 2, 27-29). Again, as in Thersites' reiteration of all being 'War and Lechery', love and war are coupled metaphorically. Troilus's overwhelming sexual infatuation with Cressida is entirely self-centered, focusing on the hazards of the commitment. As Pandarus and Cressida enter, the dialogue of the two lovers and their go-between becomes a cacophony of three radically diverging discourses: that of the hyperbolical, narcissistic poseur lover, the sleazy salesmanship of the pimp, and the confused and unsophisticated, but basically sincere discourse of a not very romantic woman in love and out of her depth. The reading of this scene, it seems to me, is the key to an understanding of the entire play. The parameters of authorization and authorial sympathies involved in the central love plot, or indeed the lack of the same, are largely determined by how this scene is read. Troilus and Cressida are indeed 'reluctant lovers', their first conversation being about the 'monstruosity in love', an exchange, interestingly, in prose:

> *Troil.*   ... when we vow to weep seas, live in fire, eat rocks, tame tigers; thinking it harder for our mistress to devise imposition enough than for us to undergo any difficulty imposed. This is the monstruosity in love, lady: that the will is infinite, and the execution confined: that the desire is boundless, and the act a slave to limit.
>
> *Cress.*   They say all lovers swear more performance than they are able, and yet reserve an ability that they never perform: vowing more than the perfection of ten, and discharging less than the tenth

	part of one. They that have the voice of lions and the act of hares, are they not monsters?
Troil.	Are there such? Such are not we: praise us as we are tasted, allow us as we prove.... Few words to fair faith: Troilus shall be such to Cressid as what envy can say worst shall be a mock for his truth, and what truth can bespeak truest, not truer than Troilus.

(III, 2, 75-97)

Pandarus' contribution to the conversation is strictly from the point of a view of a physical sexual transaction about to be carried out:

Cress.	Well, uncle, what folly I commit, I dedicate to you.
Pand.	I thank you for that: if my lord get a boy of you, you'll give him me. Be true to my lord: if he flinch, chide me for it.
Troil.	You know now your hostages: your uncle's word, and my firm faith.

So Troilus, however hyperbolical his rhetoric, is clearly a knowing part of this physical transaction. He is not in this scene elevated to a higher plane than Pandarus and Cressida, and his subsequent reactions to Cressida's 'betrayal' should be seen in this light. Indeed, Cressida in the following exchange seems the more sensitive of the two. She confesses her love for Troilus, and at the same time regrets exposing her true feelings like this:

> Why have I blabb'd ? Who shall be true to us
> When we are so unsecret to ourselves ? –
> But though I lov'd you well, I woo'd you not;
> And yet, good faith, I wish'd myself a man,
> Or that we women had men's privilege
> Of speaking first. (III, 2, 124-128)

Cressida asks Troilus to stop her talking, and Troilus takes this as an invitation to kiss her, and does so. Cressida is embarrassed at having brought on this kiss, and wants to leave, but Troilus keeps her back, leaping into high rhetoric again, a kind of rhetoric which by its very implications is profoundly insulting to Cressida. The scene, amazingly, ends in a meta-reflection by all three characters. Troilus, already rhapsodising on himself being 'as true as truth's simplicity', is seemingly swept on by the force of his own rhetoric:

> True swains in love shall, in the world to come,
> Approve their truth by Troilus; when their rhymes,

Full of protest, of oath and big compare,
Wants similes, truth tir'd with iteration....
'As true as Troilus' shall crown up the verse
And sanctify the numbers. (III, 2, 171-181)

In other words: the phrase 'as true as Troilus' will make superfluous any other rhetorical protestation of truth.

Cressida, in her counter to Troilus, for the only time in the play, leaves her role of unheroic 'material girl'; in her one flight of lofty rhetoric, emulating Troilus, and balancing Troilus's hyperbole, Cressida inverts the rhetorical figure used by Troilus, swearing not upon the certainty of her fidelity, but upon the impossibility of her being false:

If I be false, or swerve a hair from truth,
When time is old and hath forgot itself,
When waterdrops have worn the stones of Troy....
When they've said 'as false
As air, as water, wind, or sandy earth,
As fox to lamb, or wolf to heifer's calf,
Pard to the hind, or stepdame to her son' –
Yea, let them say, to stick the heart of falsehood,
'As false as Cressid'. (III, 2, 182-194)

Pandarus, to round off the scene, provides a prosaic and patently absurd conclusion to the two previous rhetorical flights:

Pand. If ever you prove false to one another, since I have taken such pains to bring you together, let all pitiful goers-between be called to the world's end after my name: call them all Pandars: let all constant men be Troiluses, all false women Cressids, and all brokers-between Pandars. Say 'Amen'.

Troil. Amen.
Cress. Amen.
Pand. Amen. Whereupon I will show you a chamber with a bed, which bed, because it shall not speak of your pretty encounters, press it to death. Away. [Exeunt Troilus and Cressida]
And Cupid, grant all tongue-tied maidens here
Bed, chamber, pander to provide this gear!   (III, 2, 197-210)

Pandarus totally ignores the rhetorical hedging by Troilus and Cressida around the theme of sex, expeditiously sending the two would-be lovers off to bed. Indeed, his finishing remark indicates that it is neither virtue nor modesty which has prevented Cressida from making love to Troilus any sooner than this, it is simply her being 'tongue-tied'.

The absurdity of the conclusion to the arguments of the two lovers, of course, lies in Pandarus' picking up on the characters' *themes* of constancy, falsehood and going-between, rather than on their *arguments*. After all, why should 'all constant men be Troilus' if Troilus turned out to be the false one? Pandarus, however, is not concerned with being logical, but with being *ana*logical. He is concerned with the analogy between the rhetorical preoccupations of the characters and their historical reputation. Pandarus, in other words, like Troilus and Cressida, is hovering between a *diegetic* and *meta-diegetic* role; he, like them, is speaking as a character inside the play, promoting the action, as well as speaking as a chorus outside the action, from a contemporary position, with the benefit of hindsight – since, after all, these are the attributes that have traditionally been applied to the three characters. But what is the function of this Brechtian alienation effect, of having characters make tongue-in-cheek references to their own subsequent reputation in literary history? What is it about Troilus and Cressida that invites Shakespeare to treat them differently than other historical characters, such as Julius Caesar, Cleopatra, or Richard III, who also had become characters with a name recognition and a 'life' beyond their specific fictional embodiments? The answer, which lies beyond the confines of this essay, is to be sought both in the 'reception history' of Homer in general and Troilus and Cressida in particular, from Chaucer to Chapman's contemporary translations of Homer. That history, combined of course with what, in part, I have been trying to do in the above analysis, a consideration of the 'form and pressure' Shakespeare was exposed to at the time of writing *Troilus and Cressida*.

Notes

All references are to the Arden edition of *Troilus and Cressida*, ed. by Kenneth Palmer (Methuen: 1982).

[1] Annabel Patterson, "The Very Age and Body of the Time His Form and Pressure", in *Shakespeare and Deconstruction*, New York: Peter Lang, 1988, ed. by G. D. Atkins and D.M. Bergeron, p. 65.
[2] See Michael Bristol, *Carnival and Theater*, London: Methuen, 1985, ch. 7, for an extended historical treatment of the author function.
[3] See Geoffrey Bullough, *Narrative and Dramatic Sources of Shakespeare*, London: Routledge and Kegan Paul, 1966, Vol IV, pp. 98-100. Bullough speculates (99-100):

'Any conclusion about the relationship between this play and Shakespeare's must be tentative. But the Admiral's piece was probably written before *Troilus and Cressida*, and the parallels in structure and content are close enough to suggest that Shakespeare conceived his play as a "realistic" answer to the unsophisticated mixture of epic and didactic sentiment likely to have characterized the piece by Dekker and Chettle.'

[4] Notably *Merchant of Venice*, V, i, 14-16, *As You Like It*, IV, 1, 96-100, and *Much Ado about Nothing*, V, 2, 30, but also *Taming of the Shrew, Merry Wives of Windsor, Henry V*, and *Twelfth Night*.

[5] *Troilus and Cressida*, ed. K. Palmer (London: Routledge, 1982) p. 125

[6] Jonathan Bate, in his book *The Genius of Shakespeare* (Picador: 1997), relishes the irony of the use of this speech made in 1994 by Michael Portillo, then Chief Secretary to the Treasury in the Thatcher government, as a criticism of those who had become cynical about ' traditional British values', Bate's point being that 'there could be no better word than "cynical" for Shakespeare's representation in *Troilus and Cressida* of traditional codes and values' (p. 189).

[7] See W.A. Armstrong in *Shakespeare Studies* 7 (1954), pp. 82-89, and A.J. Gurr, *Shakespeare Studies*, 16 (1963), pp. 95-101.

SOILING THE PAGE, DAUBING THE WALL:
A READING OF *HENRY THE FOURTH, PART ONE*, 1.1. 1-65

Charles Lock

'Literature' has long been under suspicion. The New Historicists would make no essential difference within the field of writing, or even within discourse: high literature enjoyed no privileged status, beyond that (presumably) of occasioning the search for analogues in neglected and minor forms. The tendency was to assimilate literature to discourse, and to treat all utterance as of a kind. Discourse became the term no longer in question, and utterance its normative instantiation.

The early modern period has been the playground of New Historicism, not least because the very uncertainty of that compound modifier – 'early modern' – points to an instability, to the recognition of the felt absence of such an essence as might lie concealed within 'the Elizabethan Age' or 'the English Renaissance' or 'Reformation' (even, these days, in the plural). 'Early modern' has always confessed its vagueness, and flaunted its licence to trespass.

The dominance of discourse involved the occlusion not only of 'literature' but also of the materiality of writing: discourse is what flows, and all signs have the power of signifying by virtue of their being in circulation. The model of circulation usefully challenged the fixity and monumentality of the literary text. However, it has also obstructed the application to early modern culture of the findings of grammatology. The model of circulation follows the voice; the notion of discourse can hardly survive attention to the materiality of the graphic. Voice, assuming writing to serve its purposes alone, finds the conspicuously graphic to be recalcitrant; matter snags discourse, tangles the eye, makes mute. Only in recent years have scholars of the early modern acknowledged that writing matters; that there is more to the discursive economy than the distinction between print and manuscript. This is not to say that that distinction has not repaid our attention, as it manifestly has in the works of, among others, Harold Love and H.R. Woudhuysen;[1] rather that, as a distinction, it assumes that both print and script share a function and a purpose, to be circulated, and that whatever is inked has been inked to be read, that is, to be voiced. The grammatological holds, rather, that writing is not merely the servant of voice, an instrument to convey voice across distance: writing is most itself, most graphic, when it does what the voice cannot do. The most stringent reading is that which brings out those semiotic properties of writing that bear no witness to voice, nor recognize allegiance to, or dependence on, the phonetic.

To acknowledge that writing matters is not just to admit that voice can be disparately borne by manuscript or print, but to reckon with the semiotic values and functions of writing that are entirely independent of speech. In a book of 1990 Jonathan Goldberg examined what he called *Writing Matter*, which is largely concerned with the pedagogics of literacy, how the hands of the young were taught to form their letters, how a grammar of legibility was achieved.[2] The grammatological has made a further, even (to scratch a term) incisive, incursion into the early modern with Juliet Fleming's *Graffiti and the Writing Arts of Early Modern England* (2001). Though brief, this is the first study to take into account the varieties of surfaces on which scribes might exercise their arts. That poems have been scratched on windows and on goblets has always been known: among the authors of such have been Raleigh, Donne and Queen Elizabeth. Names have been scratched on any surface: some, of Fellows attested in the 1570s, still survive at the back of a fireplace in St. John's College, Cambridge. The stately homes of England are full of such scribal relics, hitherto considered of merely incidental or anecdotal interest. As Juliet Fleming points out, most historians explain the presence of graffiti by reference to children, as if graffiti should be assigned the same low status then as it holds now. For Fleming, however, paper, being expensive, 'was not necessarily the most obvious, or suitable, medium for writing.'[3] Other materials formed a more accessible and appropriate ground for figuration. And figuration includes not only letters and numerals, but also images and abstract designs and patterns: these would often be intertwined or imbricated, and we ought not to separate the letters as text from the unlettered context, their configuration. As signs, figures need to be read.

We have always been told that, at the Reformation, the images in the churches were destroyed by a covering of whitewash. However, as Eamon Duffy has noted, in *The Stripping of the Altars* (1992), whitewashing was already known to be reversible: images were covered not to destroy them, but in order to preserve them in the hope of more tolerant times.[4] Whitewash ensured that the wall would be a most practical surface: unlike paper, it could be reused simply by applying another layer; and what was now hidden beneath that layer could always be recovered: that is to say, uncovered. Thus Fleming argues that drawing and writing on walls was widely practised in Elizabethan and Jacobean England; that it was sanctioned there in ways that are foreign to ourselves, and troubling to the categories within which we recognize graffiti; and that this is something that we have not cared to know about the age of Shakespeare.[5]

The anecdotal evidence is there, from Montaigne, Coryate, Ann Clifford and others, that it was common practice to draw or write or scribble figures or words, images or numerals, on the wall, with coal or marking stones of red ochre or lead graphite. More elaborately, mottos and proverbs would be painted on the walls of houses, interior and exterior. The practice is still widespread across central Europe, from the Alps to the Carpathians, and some comparative study might enable us to understand the process, architectural, stylistic, ideological, by which the practice fell into disuse elsewhere. Theology does not seem to have been a factor, for both Luther and Calvin encouraged the painting of words on walls. The Deuteronomist exhorts us that these words – 'The Lord our God is one Lord: And thou shalt love the Lord thy God with all thine heart, and with all thy soul, and with all thy might' – 'shall be in thine heart'; and he also commands that 'thou shalt write them upon the posts of thy house, and on thy gates.' (Deut. 6: 4-9 & 11:20) Luther saw no reason to restrict the injunction to those words, and imagined that all the words of the Bible could be 'painted on houses, on the outside and the inside, so that all can see it'; Calvin was more concerned with the Law: 'Let us have Gods lawe written, let us have the sayings of it painted on our walls.'[6]

A moral imperative is ascribed, by George Herbert, to the wall itself: 'Even the walls are not idle, but something is written or painted there which may excite the reader to a thought of piety.'[7] What do survive in countless churches are the Tables of the Law, presumably because the sanctions of the Ten Commandments, being lettered, defy iconoclasm; within consecrated spaces they have also resisted secular pressures. The blankness of walls in church, so common since, and so pure, respectable and, one assumes, conducive to thoughts of piety, would have been then the object of proverbial wit: 'A white wall is a fool's book' or, in Herbert's words, 'A white wall is the paper of a fool.'[8] A white wall is a sign not of cleanness, but of the complete absence of literacy, of one's incapacity to hold any implement capable of leaving a mark or a stain. And such whiteness is not pure, for it presents no obstacle to the temptation to think idle and unprofitable thoughts.

Fleming has made a good case for her argument not only that walls were written on, but that 'the bulk of early modern writing was written on walls': 'the whitewashed domestic wall' is 'the primary scene of writing in early modern England.'[9] This has very far-reaching implications for our understanding of its 'literature', and it challenges us to recover appropriate or adequate modes of reading.

Whiteness presents temptation, does not concentrate the mind on pious thoughts or a wise saw. A mark, a stain, a trace, is thus evidence not of dirt or ill-discipline, but proof rather that one's hands have not been idle. We must learn not to ignore stains, but to read them.

In particular, it is the word *soil* that here begs our notice. Fleming's book suggests a way in which the word might be seen, and seen to make its mark. In Shakespeare we find many samples of the soil that belongs to the nation, that defines the land, that piece of land to which one might be native; and there is also the soiling that leaves marks and stains. *Soil* as a noun can be distinguished between that which takes the definite article, 'the soil,' and that which takes none, 'soil'. *Soil* as a countable noun giving 'a soil' will refer either to a parcel of land or to a particular sort of mulch: as in 'a fertile soil' or 'a soil poor in humus': in modern usage the latter sense of 'a soil' is almost exclusive. The most recent citation in the Oxford English Dictionary for 'a soil' as in 'purchase a soil' is from 1797, and seems then to have been already archaic. 'The earth or ground; the face or surface of the earth' is the *OED's* gloss on soil as noun in its first, uncountable sense, and Holofernes is cited from *Love's Labour's Lost*: 'falleth like a crab on the face of terra, the soil, the land, the earth.' (IV ii 6-7) Satan engages in a similar if not quite so synonymously appositional series: 'Is this the region, this the soil, the clime...?' (*Paradise Lost*, I, 242)

The word *soil* in this earthy sense enters English through Anglo-Norman and is derived from Latin *solum*; the Latin word gives rise to two words in modern French, *sol* (floor) and *seuil* (threshold). *Klein's Comprehensive Etymological Dictionary of the English Language* (s.v. soil, n.) explains: 'The sense development of French *seuil*, "threshold", is due to the influence of L. *solea*, "sole of the foot" which is related to *solum*, ground.' Where there is a flat surface on a horizontal plane, another flat surface can rest. The soil is thus, precisely, in Holofernes' phrase, the 'face of terra'. The threshold is, etymologically, the treading place, the place of contact between surfaces, the site of horizontal contiguity. And by metonymy, the *solum* (ground) and the *solea* (sole) are named for each other: in English the sole of our boots leaves its print in the soil. The soil is thus the surface, all of the land that one can see; it therefore stands by contiguity for the depth of the land. The analytic quality of 'subsoil' betrays a certain anxiety over whether the word *soil* should properly denote surface or depth: it can be traced no earlier than c. 1800, and belongs to the agronomic revolution.

The other common sense of *soil*, still in use today, is the verb, invoking dirt; it has, as a word, no common source with the soil that acts as a threshold between the earth and the shoe, or – as sole – between the soil and the foot. Both of these almost-monosyllabic homophones are derived from Latin, through French: making dirty, to *soil* is cognate with French *souiller*: both are cognate with Latin *suculus*, diminutive of *pig*: modern English *sow* is related, as is the verb, to *sully*.

The two senses of *soil*, as noun and as verb, are easily connected semantically, and there are no obvious clues that the two words, homophones as well as homographs, have distinct roots. The suffix exposes *dent-al* or *dent-ist* as Latin; the stem would thus seldom be confused with the Old English noun *dent*, resulting from a blow that mars and marks a surface. The semantic connection between *dent* and *dentist* may be close, but the suffixes on the tooth keep it distinct from the mark. (Indentation is close enough to the look of dents to cause some confusion.) Whether as verb or as noun, *soil* betrays no etymological trace in its morphology: the noun takes no suffix, the verb conjugates regularly. These preliminaries – etymological ablutions on the threshold – are required. For we are going to undertake an analysis of the soil that is abundantly evident and widely distributed over the surface of the opening scene of *Henry the Fourth, Part One*.

Yet there is still another sense of soil that needs to be distinguished before we can proceed. This sense is entirely obsolete and unfamiliar to us, though it was common in the 16th century. Such a *soil* is glossed by OED (s.v. soil sb. 3) as 'a miry or muddy place used by a wild boar for wallowing in' and 'a pool or stretch of water, used as a refuge by a hunted deer or other animal.' And in this sense the word is, according to the OED, derived from *soil* as a verb, that is, to make dirty. The shift from 'miry or muddy place' to 'pool or stretch of water' is more than a shift; it is a reversal of sense in the manner of what in Latin rhetoric was termed the principle of *lucus a non lucendo*: the grove (*lucus*) is named for the light because there is no light within it. A deer 'taking soil within a flood', cited from 1613, suggests that the hunted animal seeks refuge in a fast-moving stream. Drayton's *Poly-Olbion* (1612: xiii, 137) confirms the sense of refreshment and security for which this soil is sought: 'The noble, stately deer ... Doth beat the brooks and ponds for sweet refreshing soil'. By 1674 the oddity of the word in this sense is registered: 'The last Refuge of a Hart sorely hunted is the Water (which, according to the Art, is called the Soil).' Insistently and almost exclusively, this third sense of soil appears to be used in treatises on hunting, with references only to the hunted beast, almost always the deer.

Henry the Fourth, Part One is from its opening lines much concerned with the nature of land, the relationship between nation and language, between nativity and soil:

> So shaken as we are, so wan with care,
> Find we a time for frighted peace to pant
> And breathe short-winded accents of new broils
> To be commenced in strands afar remote:
> No more the thirsty entrance of this soil
> Shall daub her lips with her own children's blood,
> No more shall trenching war channel her fields
> Nor bruise her flourets with the armed hooves
> Of hostile paces: those opposed eyes,
> Which like the meteors of a troubled heaven,
> All of one nature, of one substance bred,
> Did lately meet in the intestine shock
> And furious close of civil butchery,
> Shall now in mutual wellbeseeming ranks
> March all one way, and be no more oppos'd
> Against acquaintance, kindred and allies.

We stay with the punctuation of the First Quarto (1598), which is generally preserved through all the quartos. This importantly makes the first sentence run for sixteen lines, catching or creating the accents of a short-winded speaker, a king less in pursuit than on the run. The Folio puts a point in the middle of the ninth line, after 'hostile paces'. The Fifth Quarto of 1613 gives a capital P to a personified *Peace*, as do the sixth and seventh Quartos, of 1622 and 1632; the First Folio (1623) confirms *Peace*, though the Eighth Quarto of 1639 reverts to lower-case *peace*. Modern editors tend to put *peace* in lower-case; more damagingly, they divide up these sixteen lines according, it would seem, to the respiratory and syntactic expectations of modern actors and readers.

A breathless king speaks of 'frighted Peace' as panting and short-winded. Peace is the hunted deer, given 'a time' (found by King Henry) to speak now of further broils, occurring on strands remote. This is good news for the peace of the kingdom, for it means that civil strife will be replaced by war against a foreign enemy. 'No more the thirsty entrance of this soil Shall daub her lips...': soil with 'this' indicates that parcel of soil which can be purchased, or ruled over. Its thirsty entrance is often glossed in terms of a medieval wall-painting showing the Last Judgment: to the left of the chancel arch the damned are being consumed by Hell figured as a great red gaping mouth. Yet in the context of the hunted animal, 'this soil' might also work contrastively to its usual sense: what ought to provide refuge and refreshment is now a place of death: 'shall daub her lips with her own children's blood'. The hunted animal's thirst for water ('which, according to the Art, is called the Soil') is thus met by the parodic and reciprocal blood-thirst of the soil, native to those it consumes.

All this takes some working out, not least the link between Henry, Peace and the figured but unspoken deer: by heraldry, displayed on a banner or other iconic device, the deer can be made visible in the theatre even though it is not explicitly named. However, it is implicitly present: Henry's verb 'to pant', emphatically at the line-end, echoes Psalm 42, 'As the hart panteth after the water brooks, so panteth my soul after thee, O God. My soul thirsteth for God….' (Citing from the Authorized Version; 'pants' is not used in the Book of Common Prayer (1549) but is in the Geneva Bible (1560).) Nothing pants as a hart does. Thus, in returning to 'this soil', the deer, expecting refuge and refreshment, finds blood. This hart represents Peace, and is therefore personified as female: her lips are daubed with her own children's blood. A daub might suggest modern graffiti, as the word is often used dismissively of modern art: however, what is properly and normally daubed is whitewash. The primary definition of the verb *daub* in the OED reads: 'In building, etc.: To coat or cover (a wall or building) with a layer of plaster, mortar, clay, or the like.' The sense had developed so as also to indicate dirt or mess by the late 16th century, and is even applied to poor paintings by Dryden's time. *Daub* can only have extended its applications by forgetting its etymology: the word comes through French *dauber* from Latin *dealbare*, 'to make white, to whitewash'. To be daubed with blood is to rehearse the arch and knowing contradiction of the word's senses as expressed in the Nurse's lament over Tybalt:

> A piteous corpse, a bloody piteous corpse –
> Pale, pale as ashes, all bedaubed in blood. (Rom. 3.2.55)

We are to be amused at the Nurse's rhetoric, and yet we might also suppose that Tybalt's corpse *is* both pale and bloody, like a white wall which has been daubed, covered over, with blood.

We must move apace, lest we be detained by each word, snagged at every point. 'Armed hooves Of hostile paces' gives us that contiguity of hoof striking earth, the horseshoe (the sole) leaving its struck traces in the soil.

'As far as to the sepulchre of Christ' must suggest the whitewashing of crimes; both Henry's, and that which makes 'whited' (Matt. 23:27) the proverbial modifier of almost any sepulchre. There is, in Henry's plan, a transgression of the borders of the national soil, and a determination to get 'as far as to' which suggests all sorts of anxieties about the threshold: will he seize the sepulchre, or enter therein? Echoing 'armed hooves', but entirely changing the sense and etymology of the word: now the *arms* (as limbs) of the English soldiers will have been 'moulded in their mothers' womb', and it is the arms which will do the running:

> To chase these pagans in those holy fields
> Over whose acres walkt those blessed feet
> Which 1400 years ago were nailed
> For our advantage on the bitter cross.

Pagans are those who live in the countryside, whose fields are therefore not holy; and they render unholy the fields that ought to be holy. (These fields are unlike those in England, now channelled by trenching war, the blood running in the furrows to no redemptive end.) The play of deixis, of *these* and *those*, suggests a visual switch between what is at a distance and what is near at hand: as though 'these pagans' could be pictured, and indicated by a gesture of Henry's. Fields and acres seem to eschew the expected words 'land' or 'soil'. The Holy Land had long been (from the Latin) a standard phrase; pilgrims would return with a piece of its soil as a relic. (Note that all early Quartos give the number of years in numerals, while all modern editions provide words: those numerals can give pause to the tongue.)

From 'armed hooves' we have gone to arms moulded, and now, as a synecdoche of the incarnate Christ, to 'those blessed feet'. And it is those feet that, by walking over the acres of those fields, made them holy. Sole makes a mark on the soil, makes land holy. These feet are surely unshod, for it is exactly as they walked that they are nailed. Not nailed *to* but nailed *on* the bitter cross. That *on* establishes the contiguity of surfaces: as the feet sanctified the land, so it is, by synecdoche, the feet that make the cross holy, as well as bitter. Blessed feet, as every English speaker would still have known, are also wounded feet, feet daubed with blood.

This supremely devotional, even devout passage – hardly matched elsewhere in Shakespeare – is shown to be itself something of a whited sepulchre when the King announces, on hearing only the tidings from Wales, that they must cause him to 'Brake off our business for the Holy Land'. Not *in*, or *at* or *with*, but *for*, as though this were business being undertaken for the sake of the Holy Land. It would be good to know more of the function of *for* in the phrase 'business for', and whether it picks up what we hear (perhaps erroneously) as the commercial note of 'For our advantage'.

News from Wales is quickly matched by that from the North, of a battle that occurs 'On Holy-rood day', the Feast (September 14) kept in honour of the Empress Helen's 'Invention of the True Cross' in Jerusalem c. 330, without which 'invention' there would have been no tradition of pilgrimage to the Holy Land, nor any interest among Christians in occupying that territory.[10] As Westmorland is explaining why he cannot tell the outcome of the battle at Holmedon, the King welcomes Sir Walter Blunt, introduces him, or his name, onstage. The staging is highly enigmatic, for it is not clear whether or not Blunt enters at this point, whether he has been seen approaching on horseback, or whether the King has been keeping to himself the news that Blunt had brought some time ago.[11] If we suppose the latter, Blunt is only figuratively 'here':

> Here is a dear, a true industrious friend,
> Sir Walter Blunt, new lighted from his horse,
> Stained with the variation of each soil
> Betwixt that Holmedon and this seat of ours.[12]

This is the second occurrence of the word *soil* in the play: 'each soil' indicates that soil is countable, hence in this context presumably a piece or parcel of soil, rather than a place of refuge and refreshment. There is no doubt plenty of variation in the soil between London and Northumberland, but one must ask how each soil could be included – and identified – among the stains. (The effect is quite different from the general dirt of, say, Falstaff's 'To stand stained with travel' (H42, 5.5.24).) One will then ask a grammatical question: whether it is Sir Walter or his horse that has been so stained. All early printings have a comma after horse. If Sir Walter is actually present, we should suppose that he is seen to have newly alighted offstage. Few things Shakespearean are certain, but a horse onstage would have been a matter for the record: 'Think, when we talk of horses, that you see them.' (H5 Pr. 26). If Blunt is present, it must be Blunt who is stained. If, however, Sir Walter is not 'here', there is no way of deciding whether it is Blunt or his horse who is stained; we need not decide, for there will be no staging of our decision, and the pointing would anyway allow both man and horse to be stained.

The line fascinates because it is – to the best of my recollection – unlike anything else before the late nineteenth century. Before, let us say, the opening of Thomas Hardy's *The Mayor of Casterbridge* (1886):

> ... They were plainly but not ill clad, though the thick hoar of dust which had accumulated on their shoes and garments from an obviously long journey....

Or, more dazzlingly to display the forensic powers of eyesight, Sherlock Holmes:

> 'You have come up from the south-west, I see.'
> 'Yes, from Horsham.'
> 'That clay and chalk mixture which I see upon your toe-caps is quite distinctive.'

Or:

> 'You must have started early, and yet you had a good drive in a dog-cart, along heavy roads, before you reached the station.'
> The lady gave a violent start....
> 'There is no mystery, my dear madam.... The left arm of your jacket is spattered with mud in no less than seven places. The marks are perfectly fresh. There is no vehicle save a dog-cart which throws up mud in that way....'[13]

Narrative fiction is the literary mode for such displays: we trust the narrator, and we do not ask to count those seven spattered places ourselves. The theatre is quite the wrong place, at least onstage. Offstage it would be possible, either as a matter of narration, or for a character onstage to make a remark about what can be seen offstage, and seen only by those onstage, not by the audience. The enigma of Blunt is thus peculiarly heightened by the way in which he or his horse are so analytically described, by a monarch who may have pretensions to sovereign vision, but who makes no claims to special arts of observation or detection.

To stain is to soil, yet the soil that stains has nothing to do (etymologically) with the action of soiling. Henry's line plays with the variation in the word *soil*: between the noun for that which lies between Holmedon and London, and the verb for the action of staining. If, encouraged by Juliet Fleming, one thinks of the positive value of staining, and of the way in which any early modern surface is susceptible to writing, one might speculate that something strange is going on. The strangeness, however, is in the text: we speculate only over its sense. Might 'new lighted' offer us another pun, asking us to look at Blunt or his horse under a new light (as all our yesterdays have lighted fools)? The *from* in the verbal phrase 'lighted from' of course preserves the sense of motion, that Blunt is dismounting. But we should consider that something visual, and visible, might be happening: some optical business that would justify the King's extraordinary words, and that might even explain how Blunt could be at once present and absent.

This paper, though not blank, offers no solution, but looks with hope at space and spaces. There is a poem illustrated in Fleming, from a book of emblems printed in Cambridge in 1592. The poem is about faithful pastors being fishers of men, and the verses are laid out on the page in blocks, chessboard-wise, thus resembling the cords and openings of a fishing-net. As writing is made to conform to the visual expectations of linearity – as, at the bidding of the voice, the textile is unraveled into the thread of the discourse – so shape poems fade away; they come back in the late nineteenth century, with Lewis Carroll and Mallarmé. Between c. 1650 and c. 1850 readers were expected to pay no attention to white spaces. (In *Tristram Shandy* their presence signals only, and most plainly, the absurd.) Yet in the early modern period white spaces would always be significant, even if only as the fool's paper. Were there, perhaps, white spaces in the Elizabethan theatre, walls to be daubed? Was there a whited ground, entirely occluded to the modern eye, on which the eyes of Shakespeare's contemporaries could read stains, marks, traces, prints of hands and feet? On which the audience could see variations in soil, be witness to deeds of soiling?

Something here is not quite white. Whatever the stain, it ought to provoke us to read: our task is to recover and uncover the reading of what has been neglected: whatever signs defy the voice. Despite the treacherous nature of editorial practice, 'the words on the page' have proved a relatively safe shelter. Our reading of words has ignored whatever graphic marks might have been displaced from their proper site in modernity: the page. And it has ignored those figurations, actual and potential, that the voice cannot recognize or articulate.

For any who would treat this plea for a white wall (and for all the marks thereon) as the paper of a fool, one can respond only in muteness, pointing to a short story – set in early modern Portugal – by Isak Dinesen, 'The Blank Page'. Lacking mark or stain or soil, that white surface does need a voice to tell its tale.

Notes

[1] See Harold Love, *Scribal Publication in Seventeenth Century England* (Oxford: 1993); H. R. Woudhuysen, *Sir Philip Sidney and the Circulation of Manuscripts, 1558-1640* (Oxford: 1996).

2. Jonathan Goldberg, *Writing Matter: From the Hands of the English Renaissance* (Stanford CA: 1990).
3. Juliet Fleming, *Graffiti and the Writing Arts of Early Modern England* (London: Reaktion, 2001), p. 10.
4. Eamon Duffy, *The Stripping of the Altars: Traditional Religion in England 1400-1580* (New Haven CT: 1992), p. 583; cited in Fleming, p. 77.
5. Fleming, p. 29.
6. Cited in Fleming, p. 65.
7. Cited in Fleming, p. 58.
8. Cited in Fleming, p. 49.
9. Fleming, p. 50.
10. See Charles Lock, 'Bowing Down to Wood and Stone: One Way to be a Pilgrim' in S. Coleman and J. Elsner, eds., *Pilgrim Voices: Narrative and Authorship in Christian Pilgrimage* (New York, Oxford: Berghahn, 2003), 110-32 (119).
11. The problem of Blunt's presence or absence is glossed over by many editors and commentators; exceptional candour is shown by David Bevington in his edition of *Henry IV, Part 1* (1987) in the Oxford Shakespeare: see note to 1.1.62-3.
12. Q1 (1598) reads 'Here is deere, a true industrious friend', as if the word suppressed in so much panting insisted now on being spelt as pronounced. Q2 (1599) corrects to 'deare' but does not add the indefinite article. Q5 (1613) introduces 'a deare'. F1 has 'a deere'.
13. See 'The Five Orange Pips' and 'The Speckled Band' in A. Conan Doyle, *The Adventures of Sherlock Holmes* (London: 1893), p. 109, p. 183. On the forensic aspect of vision in Hardy, see Charles Lock, 'Hardy and the Critics' in P. Mallett, ed., *Palgrave Advances in Thomas Hardy Studies* (Houndmills: 2004), pp. 32-34.

'NOW IS HE TURNED ORTHOGRAPHY': ON SILENCE AND WRITING

Søs Haugaard

Physical representation – the embodiment of a role – might aptly be termed the idiom of the language of the theatre. By the same token, dramatic characters would then constitute the idiom of the dramatic text on the page and thus invite analysis of their makeup, of their relationship with the text as a whole, and with other 'idioms'. The plays in which we find the characters dealt with in this article are *Much Ado About Nothing, Romeo and Juliet, King Henry V* and *Othello*.

In the dedication to *The Sonnets* we hear of 'that eternity promised by our ever-living poet'. It is tempting, with this in mind, to treat the poet of *The Sonnets* as a dramatic character introduced to us by the 'playwright' in this fashion. So, in the following, I shall attempt to read the sonnet sequence as a kind of play, where all the lines are spoken by one character. This, I hope, could throw new light on the dramatic fabric of *The Sonnets*.

Theatre in performance will always raise issues of deixis,[1] as 'that bare vowel "I"'(*Rom*. III.ii.47)[2] is spoken by a different 'I', namely the actor embodying the role. In the case of the early modern theatre, it must be assumed that physical and material conditions of the bare stage prompted a need for explicit verbalisation of the actor's embodiment of the role.[3]

Neither on the page, nor in performance, can a character then be said to have *presence* in an early modern play until he has spoken.[4] While language, manner and costume all may be suggestive of the character's identity and social status, his specific identity – his name, his place in social and familial structures etc, – can only be established when he is addressed by or referred to by other characters. This theatrical practice, which requires you to speak in order to exist and others to speak to you or about you in order for you to have an identity, lends great metaphoric potential to *silence*.

Although the practicalities of the theatre do not play tyrant to lyrical poetry, aesthetic convention dictates that in that genre only one voice speaks. In England in the last decade of the sixteenth century, the intimacy and privacy of the lyrical mode would not only have been a question of *mood* in its literary sense, but most probably also a fact of the circumstances under which sonnet sequences were read, passed as they were from hand to hand and not always meant for publication.

The question of presence and absence in lyrical poetry is intriguing. Even when there is a *here and now* in the poem, in which the speaker exists, it is ambiguous if the addressee is "absent" or "present" in principle.

If we suppose that a character's presence in a Shakespeare play is only a fact when he speaks, scenes where one character requests a sign of life from another acquire special significance. In *Romeo and Juliet*, Mercutio, looking for his friend, calls out 'Romeo! Humours! Madman! Passion! Lover! / Appear thou in the likeness of a sigh, / Speak but one rhyme and I am satisfied.' (*Rom*. II.i. 7-9). In the imagined darkness of the scene, Mercutio cannot find Romeo unless he speaks. The reader of the text is of course in the same kind of darkness.

Let us compare this to the last act of *Othello*, where Emilia finds the lifeless Desdemona and cries out : 'Help, help, ho, help! O lady, speak again, / Sweet Desdemona, O sweet mistress, speak!' (*Oth*. V.ii.119-120) The proof of life that Emilia longs for is significant: we understand that silence means death. Indeed, when Emilia asks: 'O, who hath done/This deed?' Desdemona replies: 'Nobody. I myself. Farewell!' (*Oth*. V.ii.121-122) Desdemona is no longer 'anybody'; she is no longer in the play once she has fallen silent.

By way of contrast, Emilia refuses to be silenced. 'I will not charm my tongue, I am bound to speak,' (*Oth*. V.ii.180) she says when told to be quiet. Characteristically, her dying words are:

> I will play the swan
> And die in music. Willow, willow, willow.
> – Moor, she was chaste, she loved thee, cruel Moor,
> So come my soul to bliss as I speak true!
> So speaking as I think, alas, I die. (*Oth*. V.ii.245-249)

So, unlike Desdemona, who is annihilated as a character by her silence, Emilia dies still speaking.

In the same play the once so dangerously eloquent Cassio is also destroyed by his own – alcohol-induced – silence. After the first fateful drink, Cassio says 'I can stand well enough, and I speak well enough' (*Oth*. II.iii.11-112). When Othello arrives on the scene, however, Cassio has lost that very property: 'I cannot speak' (*Oth*. II.iii.185). Cassio's inability to speak renders him incapable of action at a crucial point in the dramatic development and consequently destroys him.

We may wonder, however, if a character's silence necessarily means that he is dead or powerless. In *Much Ado*, for instance, Don John soliloquises: 'If I had my mouth I would bite' (*Ado* I.iii.32-33), but, unlike Cassio, Don John is capable of taking charge of the situation even without his mouth, and he is able to stage the 'seeming truth of Hero's disloyalty' (*Ado* II. ii. 48). The evidence that Don John and Borachio are able to produce is like a dumb show, where only two words, two names, are spoken (*Ado* II. ii. 40-49). It is worth noting that it is the duped characters, Claudio especially, who find the words for Don John's mimed lie. So it seems that Don John is capable of controlling the situation in spite of his silence.

Iago's silence, on the other hand, is ambiguous. When Othello demands to know why he has destroyed him, Iago says: 'Demand me nothing. What you know, you know. / From this time forth I never will speak word' (*Oth.* V.ii.300-301). These are in fact his last words in the play, and we may wonder if his silence spells victory or defeat.

Albeit in a very different way, Juliet's silence is equally ambiguous. In the balcony scene, Romeo says, 'She speaks, yet she says nothing. What of that? / Her eye discourses, I will answer it.' *(Rom.* II. ii. 12-13) Below I shall discuss how the human anatomy may serve as a passive medium for an inner truth or might even be an unresisting object onto which lies may be written, but Juliet's silence is clearly of a different kind. Far from allowing others to write their stories on her face or her body, she has eyes capable of discourse even when she is silent.[5]

In *The Sonnets* Shakespeare exploits the paradoxical rhetorical device of recommending plain speaking in very elaborate terms. In Sonnet 82 the poet pays tribute to plain words

> when they have devised,
> What strained touches rhetoric can lend,
> Thou truly fair, wert truly sympathized
> In true plain words, by thy true-telling friend (Sonnet 82)

Several dramatic characters in Shakespeare seem to share the poet's interest in plain words, which they brandish as more truthful than the 'strained touches'. And, as is the case with the poet of *The Sonnets,* Juliet, Othello and others demonstrate their eloquence by denying it. Juliet says:

> Conceit more rich in matter than in words
> Brags of his substance, not of ornament.
> They are but beggars that can count their worth,
> But my true love is grown to such excess
> I cannot sum up sum of half my wealth. *(Rom.* II.vi. 30-34)

Her lines evoke Cleopatra's 'There is beggary in the love that can be reckoned'

(*Ant.* I.i.15), as well as Cordelia's 'I am sure my love's / More ponderous than my tongue' (*Lr.* I. i. 77-78). Yet, unlike Cordelia, Juliet is indeed capable of heaving her heart into her mouth, and in her long soliloquy in Act III we encounter a personal lover's rhetoric, which embraces both the conventional Petrarchan rhetoric: 'Take him and cut him out in little stars, / And he will make the face of heaven so fine / That all the world will be in love with night, / And pay no worship to the garish sun.' (*Rom.* III. ii. 22-25) and plainer more personal imagery: 'Come, civil night, / Thou sober-suited matron, all in black' (*Rom.* III.ii.10-11). Juliet appears to master several rhetorical registers, including one that involves silence.

Othello, even more emphatically than Juliet, insists that he is without eloquence: 'Haply for I am black/And have not those soft parts of conversation/That chamberers have . . . .' (*Oth.* III. iii. 267-268). Othello is, it seems, a man of action, and he trusts his actions to speak for themselves: 'My services, which I have done the signiory, /Shall out-tongue his [Brabanteo's] complaints' (*Oth.* I.ii.19). Othello's condition is, however, not simply a lack of words and a – reported – competence in action. The language in which he is competent is that of war:

> . . . little of this great world can I speak
> More than pertains to feats of broil and battle,
> And therefore little shall I grace my cause
> In speaking for myself. Yet by your gracious patience,
> I will a round unvarnished tale deliver .... (*Oth.* I. iii. 87-91)

So, as well as speaking, Othello tells us how he speaks.

Although sonnet 23 deals with the same problem, here the question is not whether simple rhetoric is inherently more genuine that an ornamental style. Rather, it is a question of genuine emotion precluding verbal eloquence. The poet compares himself to 'an unperfect actor' forgetting his lines 'O'ercharg'd with burthen of mine own love's might.' Unable to speak, the poet relies on his books to be 'then the eloquence / And dumb presagers of my speaking breast.' In other words books are unable to speak, yet eloquent, and the poet's breast speaks while his tongue is silent.

The poet goes on to encourage the addressee to 'learn to read what silent love hath writ: / To hear with eyes belongs to love's fine wit.' So here the breast speaks and the tongue is silent, yet eyes can hear. We may be reminded of the eye in sonnet 152, which is indeed capable of swearing and lying.

The anxiety of being unable to write manifests itself in the poet's imagined conversations with his muse, and we find it in Sonnet 80 too: the rival poet's work might 'make me tongue-tied speaking of your fame.' Interestingly, the silence of the young man may be implicitly dealt with in line 10, 'he upon your soundless deep doth ride', with a pun on *soundless*, meaning 'without a sound' as well as 'unfathomable'.

While the poet thus displays some signs of anxiety over the prospect of being silenced, in Sonnet 83 he asserts that his silence 'shall be most my glory being dumb; / For I impair not beauty being mute.' Similarly, in Sonnet 85, the poet speaks of his 'good thoughts, whilst others write good words' and concludes the sonnet with: 'Then others, for the breath of words respect, / Me for my dumb thoughts, speaking in effect.' Like the speaking breast of Sonnet 23 and like Juliet's eyes, the thoughts in Sonnet 85 speak even though they are dumb.

In Sonnet 83 this paradox is at play when the poet states in the opening lines: 'I never saw that you did painting need, / And therefore to your fair no painting set'. The sonnet goes on to become an apology for the poet's silence, the addressee exceeds the 'barren tender of a poet's debt' and anyway 'a modern quill doth come too short'.

The poet then goes on to twist an earlier argument: The 'gilded tomb' of Sonnet 101 and the 'entombed' addressee and his 'monument' of Sonnet 81 address the paradox of death as a prerequisite for immortality. As the poet repeatedly tells us, truth might *die* in beauty, and consequently its preservation must also be its destruction. In Sonnet 83, however, the poet leaves it to his rivals who 'would give life, and bring a tomb' to bury the addressee in poetry, and the poet's own silence 'shall be most my glory being dumb'. Where the earlier argument allows the young man's beauty and the sonnets to immortalise one another, the argument that silence is the greatest tribute makes the sonnet implode or annihilate itself. Elsewhere the poet exploits the rhetorical device of comparing the object of praise to that which is not present (see below). This strategy is thus taken to a further extreme in Sonnet 83, where the sonnet itself claims not to be there at all.

The poet also explains his silence with the superfluity of words. Throughout the sonnet sequence the poet makes the claim that the young man's beauty is superior to any possible representation of it and needs no improvement or praise: 'The argument, all bare, is of more worth / Than when it hath my added praise beside!'

Viewed as a dramatic character, the poet of *The Sonnets* displays the kind of false modesty we find in Juliet and Othello, and we recognise his anxiety about 'writer's block'. Prompted by the genre's conventional claim to immortality, however, the sonneteer displays silence as the ultimate praise, in the same way that death is a prerequisite for immortality.

Consequently, the poet's occasional claim to silence while 'speaking' may well adhere to the Elizabethan fashion of paradoxes, but seen in the light of *speaking* as that which constitutes existence, it also communicates with the theme of death and immortality.

Even if only the poet, not the young man, is allowed to speak in *The Sonnets*, the poet and the young man mutually depend on one another for their existence in the text. The poet must speak to 'be there', therefore he must speak, but for that he needs a worthy subject, as is required by the genre. As the young man is 'soundless', he depends on the poet's references to his presence to be present in the text, that is in order to exist at all.

As mentioned above, the poet is seen to create a distance between the object of his description and that to which it is compared by choosing, not the thing itself, but a representation of it. This, in its own turn, raises the question of absence and presence in the *here* and *now* of the poem in relation to ekphrasis. Do the paintings or statues in question need to have any presence in the *here* and *now* of the poem, and if so how might that presence be constituted?

If we turn to Sonnet 59, we are confronted with a portrait painted in letters ('character'). If we choose to consider that a form of ekphrasis and return to the question of presence, we must conclude that letters are present beyond anything else in the text. Following that idea, the close metaphorical relationship between the young man and books, pages and writing gives him a presence in the text that he would not otherwise have.

Sonnet 5 stands out in the sonnet sequence with the way in which its neo-Platonism finds expression in metaphors drawing on the experience of mundane household tasks: 'flowers distilled, though they with winter meet, / Leese but their show; their substance still lives sweet' (Sonnet 5). In Sonnet 53 we are more directly confronted with the philosophical scope inherent in the word 'substance': 'What is your substance, whereof are you made, / That millions of strange shadows on you tend?' (Sonnet 53).

The rhetorical question expresses the poet's wonder at the young man's beauty: What matter could possibly have such an effect? And do not other beings ('shadows') appear inferior in comparison to the young man?

However, lines 3 and 4 complicate the concept of *shadows*, and, consequently, also the idea of *substance*: 'Since every one, hath every one, one shade, / And you but one, can every shadow lend'. So there is a relationship between a 'substance' and its physical manifestation, its 'shadow'. We remember the distilled flowers of Sonnet 5, which lose 'but their show' while 'their substance still lives sweet.' Quite apart from its strong Platonic connotations, 'shadow' also makes us aware of the distance between representations and that which they represent. One might say that the sonnet offers implicit ekphrasis by staging the young man as a representation – be it a pictorial or dramatic one.[6]

After dealing with the shadows, Sonnet 53 goes on to say: 'Describe Adonis, and the counterfeit / Is poorly imitated after you.' Is it the counterfeit Adonis or the description of Adonis, one wonders. At any rate, what we see here is a rhetorical device where paradoxically a thing of the past is described as a copy of a thing of the present. If we see Adonis as an ideal, rather than a figure of the past, we are faced with an even more sophisticated paradox: the very idea of beauty is only an inferior copy of the beauty of the young man.

The sonnet continues this line of thought: 'On Helen's cheek all art of beauty set, / And you in Grecian tires are painted new'. The young man's beauty is a match even for a portrait of the most beautiful woman in the history of the world. The poet thus creates a distance between the object of his description and that to which it is compared by choosing, not the thing itself, but a representation of it.

The idea of the portrait of Helen turning into a portrait of the young man in Greek costume 'painted new' adds another aspect to the existing paradox: a present beauty in the tires of the past making for a new image. The poet's overreaching bid to allow beauty to be measured in comparison with what you might call 'verbally absent' ideals is inevitably self-referential and what we may call 'meta-poetic'. It also identifies the poet as a playful braggart.

Following this line of thought, we may turn to Sonnet 106, which begins 'When in the chronicle of wasted time / I see descriptions of the fairest wights'. With its archaisms (e.g. 'wights') and phrases like 'In praise of ladies dead and lovely knights' the sonnet evokes a sense of pathos if not ridicule. However, 'I see their antique pen would have expressed / Even such a beauty as you master now.' We are given to understand that the earlier verbal representations of beauty foreshadowed the young man's beauty ('all you prefiguring'), but even they – the 'antique pens' – would prove inadequate: 'They had not skill enough your worth to sing', the poet asserts.

The poet's seeming modesty is thus undercut by the parodic representation of the poetic style of the past, and his claim to having 'eyes to wonder' but lacking 'tongues to praise' is naturally contradicted by the sonnet itself and by the entire sonnet sequence.

In this way the poet's style is indirectly compared to another, supposedly superior, style which is referred to, but not manifested, in the text. As in the Adonis example, the distance or absence of the point of comparison lends the subject of praise a sublime quality.

Such formal challenges are also found in the plays. In *Romeo and Juliet*, in what may be described as a literary equivalent to the *occupatio* of legal rhetoric, the Nurse says to Juliet, 'Though his [Romeo's] face be better than any man's, yet his leg excels all men's, and for a hand and a foot and a body, though they be not to be talked on, yet they are past compare' *(Rom.* II.v. 40-43). Romeo's body may not be worth talking about or it may be improper for the Nurse and Juliet to discuss it, but we may note how 'for a hand and a foot and a body' echoes Juliet's earlier contemplation that a name is 'nor hand nor foot / Nor arm nor face' *(Rom.* II.ii. 40-41). Where Juliet reminds us that the actual physical Romeo is separate from the name 'Romeo',[7] the Nurse suggests that Romeo's body, both in its excellence and with its shortcomings, is *there* whether or not it is 'talked on'.

The Nurse's and Juliet's acknowledgement that Romeo exists even when he is not 'talked on' at once challenges and confirms the very basis of theatre. How can a dramatic character exist except through words? On the other hand, the theatre depends on the compliance of the audience, and the play's insistence that we believe in Romeo in spite of his absence is reminiscent of the poet's showing-off in *The Sonnets*.

The distinctly physical nature of Romeo and Juliet's love for one another makes the question of physical presences all the more pressing. It is, however, not only in love that actual physical presence is crucial; this we are confronted with in *Henry V*, where the absence of a sufficient number of soldiers is at the core of the play's conflict. Indeed, as Westmorland says, 'Never king of England / Had nobles richer and more loyal subjects, / Whose hearts have left their bodies here in England / And lie pavillioned in the fields of France' (*H5* I. ii. 126-129) to which Canterbury replies: 'O let their bodies follow' (*H5* I. ii. 130). Where Juliet separates the name from the person, Westmorland undercuts 'hearts' as a metaphor for thoughts and feelings. Both lovers and warlords might be excused for being more interested in actual bodies than in abstracts such as names and 'hearts'.

Just as Romeo's body is given presence in verbal reports, dead English soldiers are allowed a striking and sensual presence in France and on the stage, when King Henry says:

> Though buried in your dunghills,
> They shall be famed, for there the sun shall greet them,
> And draw their honours reeking up to heaven,
> Leaving their earthly parts to choke your clime,
> The smell whereof shall breed a plague in France. (*H5* IV. iii. 99-103)

What is striking about this speech is not only that the English soldiers are not present with Henry when he speaks, they are barely present even in the scene he describes with the sun greeting the dead soldiers, drawing their honours 'reeking up to heaven', leaving a poisonous smell in France. Henry's description could very well deserve the epithet coined by Mercutio: 'as thin of substance as the air', but the smell stays with those who listen to him.

The insistence that certain characters exist even when absent both from the stage and from the dialogue does indeed present formal challenges. In *Much Ado* we encounter a complication of this idea. Hero's fake death is supposed to have the following effect on Claudio, according to the Friar:

> Th'idea of her life shall sweetly creep
> Into his [Claudio's] study of imagination,
> And every lovely organ of her life
> Shall come apparell'd in more precious habit,
> More moving-delicate and full of life,
> Into the eye and prospect of his soul
> Than when she liv'd indeed. (*Ado* IV. i. 224-230)

In the play, as in *The Sonnets*, beauty in art surpasses beauty in life. The 'Hero' rewritten in the study of Claudio's imagination will be lovelier and, notably, more 'full of life' than Hero was when she was 'alive'.

And the Friar's prediction does indeed come true. When Claudio realises that Hero is innocent, but still believes her to be dead, he exclaims: 'Sweet Hero! Now thy image doth appear / In the rare semblance that I lov'd it first.' (*Ado* V. i. 245-246). Hero's absence enables Claudio to see her, but the preference for the absent and therefore ideal Hero holds a threat of silencing and annihilation.

It would appear that Claudio is not alone in creating ideal versions of a loved one in the privacy of his imagination. In Sonnet 27 the poet lies sleepless in bed and sees the addressee with his 'soul's imaginary sight', whereas in Sonnet 24 the poet's eye 'hath played the painter' and 'Mine eyes have drawn thy shape'. So in this sonnet the young man is set forth as created by the poet's imagination while at the same time remaining a thing outside of the poet's self that he, the poet, can contemplate. By way of contrast the poet's eyes in Sonnet 24 are more like the eye of a camera: 'eyes this cunning want to grace their art, / They draw but what they see, know not the heart'. Taking both sonnets into account, it would seem that the poet is both creator and recorder of the young man's beauty. Both types of relationship raise issues of power.

The metaphoric potential of books in descriptions of men and their inward and outward qualities is widely exploited in Shakespeare. Thus Lady Capulet recommends Paris to Juliet saying: 'And what obscur'd in this fair volume lies, / Find written in the margent of his eyes.' *(Rom.* I.iv. 85-86). Not only does Paris's character manifest itself as writing in the play, his character, in a different sense of the word, is written in his anatomy. We may find that he shares this circumstance with Romeo, when the book metaphor appears again in Act III: on learning that Romeo has killed Tybalt, Juliet wonders 'Was ever book containing such vile matter / So fairly bound?' *(Rom.* III.ii. 83-84)

This rather simple metaphor is put to more dramatic and violent use in *Othello*, where the Moor says: 'Was this fair paper [Desdemona], this most goodly book / Made to write "whore" upon?' *(Oth.* IV.ii.72-73) As the audience will appreciate, this particular writing is false and hostile, as Desdemona has been smeared.

A similar image of writing which taints and smears white innocence appears in *Much Ado*, in which Leonato says of his traduced daughter: 'O, she [Hero] is fall'n / Into a pit of ink, that the wide sea / Hath drops too few to wash her clean again' *(Ado* IV. i. 139-141). In Hero's case we are not even sure that the ink forms letters and words; the image is overwhelming.

Blushing is another way in which a character's inner qualities may be written on his face.[8] One example is found in the balcony scene, where Juliet assures Romeo: 'Thou knowest the mask of night is on my face, / Else would a maiden blush bepaint my cheek / For that which thou hast heard me speak tonight' *(Rom.* II. ii. 85-87). So the mask conceals the truth of Juliet's modesty, which is written in her face.

But, like other forms of writing, what is written in a human face may be false. Claudio observes 'Behold how like a maid she blushes here!' *(Ado* IV. i. 33) but goes on to say: 'Comes not that blood as modest evidence /To witness simple virtue? Would you not swear, /All you that see her, that she were a maid, / By these exterior shows? But she is none.' *(Ado* IV.i.36-39) Leonato goes even further and takes the blush in Hero's cheeks as evidence of her guilt, and he asks: 'Could she here deny / The story that is printed in her blood?' *(Ado* IV.i.121-122).

We saw earlier how Paris's moral character was 'written in the margent of his eyes', yet Hero's moral flaw is 'printed' in her blood. In Leonato's outraged vocabulary 'printed' may mean 'clearly stated', but the audience, who know the truth, will acknowledge other connotations: something forcibly attached, a ready-made statement transferred onto the white paper.

In *Much Ado*, however, we also encounter an example of feeble and powerless writing. Here Benedick speaks disappointedly of how being in love has changed Claudio: 'He was wont to speak plain and to the purpose, like an honest man and a soldier, and now is he turned orthography – his words are a very fantastical banquet' (*Ado* II. iii. 18-21). Claudio's pathetic state shows us yet another twist in the tail of the multifaceted metaphor: from being a man of action, Claudio has been reduced to mere 'orthography'. In other words, he is not even a book or a page onto which something may be written or printed but simply the writing itself, which, without paper, has no physical presence.

Beatrice's wit manifests itself in her lines, but it is also frequently commented on by the other characters. Hero says she 'never yet saw a man, / How wise, how noble, young, how rarely featur'd, / But she [Beatrice] would spell him backward' (*Ado* III. i. 59-61). Beatrice has the power, it seems, to 'write' other characters and spell them in any way she likes.

Before the end of the play, however, we shall see both Beatrice and Benedick defeated by writing. This is when Hero and Claudio produce written evidence of their love for one another, and Benedick is forced to say: 'A miracle! Here's our own hands against our hearts' (*Ado* V. iv. 91-92). Dogberry's insistence that it be written down that he was called an ass further emphasises the authority of the written word.

It would appear that the dramatic characters discussed here are all powerless in the face of writing: Their true nature may transpire and be written in their eyes and faces, but, more importantly, others may write *on* them, in which case they have no more power to defend themselves than does a sheet of paper.

We have seen how the poet of *The Sonnets* and a string of characters in the plays exercise power over other characters with words: by silencing them, by redefining them in their absence and through slander. One might say that the playwright's creatures compete with him in controlling the action, as, at times, the poet of *The Sonnets* almost rambles in apparent fear of being usurped by another speaker. This strategy, one might argue, rather backfires when the poet's representation of silence as the greatest possible tribute allows the text to implode or annihilate itself.

We have also seen how silence and absence are ambiguous entities, which on the one hand leave a vacuum for other characters to define the silent or absent character; on the other, the ambiguity of silence and absence holds a subversive potential. Indeed, Don John, Juliet and to some extent Emilia, who are all at odds with the established order, have the power to be silent without being destroyed.

It would appear that Shakespeare's characters – and here I include the poet of *The Sonnets* – live in fear of being silenced, and thus annihilated, or changed by their creator or by other characters. This sense of *agon* is an impressive dramatic force, in *The Sonnets* no less than in the plays.

Notes

1. See Keir Elam, *The Semiotics of Theatre and Drama* (London: Routledge, 1980), pp. 138-148
2. All quotations from Shakespeare are from *The Arden Shakespeare*.
3. According to Allan C. Dessen, costumes and personal props would help set the scene and define the *locale*, a job otherwise left to the dialogue. See Allan C. Dessen, *Recovering Shakespeare's Theatrical Vocabulary* (Cambridge: Cambridge University Press, 1995) pp. 127-129 and pp. 150-153.
4. For an interesting discussion of the dramatic effect of silent presence and the problem of stage directions, see Allan C. Dessen, *Elizabethan Stage Conventions and Modern Interpreters* (Cambridge: Cambridge University Press, 1984), pp. 5-7.
5. For an interesting discussion of lying eyes in *The Sonnets*, see Joel Fineman, *Shakespeare's Perjured Eye*, (Berkeley: University of California Press, 1986).
6. The Elizabethan use of 'shadow' for actor is the basis of the dramatic connotations.
7. Romeo makes the same point: 'Had I it [his name] written, I would tear the word.' (*Rom.* II.ii. 57).
8. Consider for instance these lines by Sir Thomas Wyatt: 'The longe loue, that in my thought I harber, / And in my hart doth kepe his residence, / Into my face preaseth with bold pretence, / And there campeth, displaying his *banner*.' (emphasis mine) in Hyder Edward Rollins ed., *Tottel's Miscellany* (Cambridge, Massachusetts: Harvard University Press, 1966), p. 32.

WHAT HAPPENED TO *HAMLET*?
TEXT AND TRADITION

Lars Kaaber

In 1897, George Bernard Shaw wrote to Ellen Terry: 'I am certain I could make *Hamlet* a success by having it played as Shakespeare meant it.'[1] According to Shaw, nearly three centuries of stage tradition had changed the play beyond recognition.

We cannot be certain what *Hamlet* was like at the première in 1601, or that the play was ever performed 'as Shakespeare meant it'. What we know as the full *Hamlet* – *Quarto 2* and *Folio* – would certainly violate 'the two hours' traffic of our stage' and take almost four hours to perform (E.K. Chambers' estimate[2]). Even then the actors would have to speak their lines at the speed of a patter song from a Gilbert & Sullivan operetta. However, theatrical events often run up to four hours and, if we follow *Hamlet* through history, we find that most cuts are not made to save time, but rather to save the hero of the play from charges of immorality or brutality.

For all we know, the era of Betterton was the first to see a decisive division between *Hamlet* on the page and *Hamlet* on the stage. The first unkind cuts were made in 1661 by William Davenant who, although boasting that he was Shakespeare's illegitimate son,[3] subjected the plays to the most unfilial treatment. In 1693, critic Thomas Rymer applied neoclassical rules to Shakespearean tragedy and found the dramatist 'quite out of his element, his brains are turned, he raves and rambles without any coherence, any spark of reason, or any rule to control him, or any bounds to his frenzy'. Although Dryden bravely stepped in to defend the Bard, it appears that the general treatment of *Hamlet* followed Rymer's prescripts. All passages deemed defamatory to the image of Hamlet as the noble avenger were indiscriminately removed. Betterton's Prince was thus spared the ordeal of calling himself 'a dull and muddy-mettled rascal', 'a coward', 'an ass', and in IV.4, no occasions whatsoever informed against Betterton's Hamlet, or spurred his dull revenge. This particular *Quarto-2* soliloquy ('How all occasions do inform against me') was not heard again for another hundred years.

Among the passages cut in observance of Restoration morality were Laertes' advice to his sister in I.3 ('your chaste treasure open'), Hamlet's 'country matters' dialogue in the Player scene, and Ophelia's bawdy songs. Even Gertrude's delicately phrased reference to the vulgar name of the flowers in Ophelia's wreath – the Dead Men's Fingers 'that liberal shepherds give a grosser name' – was too racy. Apart from being unsavoury, the thought of a king going through the guts of a beggar was also considered improper, as was Hamlet's tirade against Danish drinking habits. Apparently, the only parts omitted for the practical purpose of shortening the play were the references to Norway. These cuts rendered Fortinbras a somewhat mysterious figure when he was nevertheless allowed to enter at the end of the tragedy. Tradition soon took care of that, and in the beginning of the 18th century the Norwegian Prince was entirely expelled from the play. He was not to return for nearly two hundred years.

Once passages or lines were cut from the tragedy the result became tradition, and it would prove a Herculean labour on the part of individual actors to restore the original text to performance. This may seem odd, since Shakespeare's full *Hamlet* has been accessible in print ever since Rowe published it in 1709, but it is partly explained by literary indolence. As Joseph Shepherd Munden said: 'I never read any book but a play, no play but one in which I myself acted, and no portion of that play but my own scenes'.[4] Instead of defending Shakespeare, men of letters often washed their hands of the whole affair and simply agreed with Hazlitt that Shakespeare's dramas should never be acted, least of all *Hamlet*.[5]

David Garrick was the next of the renowned Hamlets to wreak havoc on the text of the tragedy. It was his express desire not to leave the stage till he had 'rescued that noble play from all the rubbish of the fifth act'.[6] In 1772 he reinstated 'How all occasions do inform against me', but deprived Hamlet of his trip to England: on the verge of embarking on the ship, Garrick replaced the last lines of the soliloquy ('O, from this time forth, my thoughts be bloody or be nothing worth'), with lines of his own invention: 'O, from this time forth, my thoughts be bloody all! The hour is come! I'll fly my keepers! Sweep to my revenge!' – upon which he swept to court and arrived just in time to hear the distraught Laertes curse him for being the author of the deaths of Polonius and Ophelia. When Claudius tried to intervene in the ensuing scuffle, Garrick promptly stabbed him and was in turn skewered on Laertes' sword. Horatio then preferred to take Laertes' life rather than his own, which Garrick's Hamlet nobly prevented and, with his dying breath, the Prince commanded the two surviving youths to 'unite their virtues and calm the troubled land'.[7] Garrick contrived to get through the play from 'How all occasions' to Hamlet's death in only 215 lines, against Shakespeare's 1085. Such was the Shakespearean legacy he passed on to future generations.

However, we must consider that not only did Garrick dispense with Act V in order to restore vast parts of the previous four, he also withstood many strictures hurled at Shakespeare. The fiercest of these came in 1768 from

Voltaire who claimed that *Hamlet* seemed like the work of a drunken savage.[8] English retaliation came in 1769, in the shape of Mrs. Montagu's *Essay on the Writings and Genius of Shakespeare, with some remarks upon the misrepresentations of Mons. De Voltaire*.[9] Mrs. Montagu compared Shakespeare's 'natural sallies of passion' favourably with the 'pompous declamation' of Voltaire's *Tancred*. She demonstrated that Voltaire's attack on Shakespeare was an unethical attempt to cover up the fact that the French dramatist had borrowed profusely from the Bard: whole scenes had been looted from *Macbeth* in order to fill up Voltaire's *Mahomet*, and *Othello* had been rewritten into *Zaïre*.

Among the English detractors of Shakespearean drama in Garrick's day we find George Steevens, who confessed that he could never be 'reconciled to tragicomedy'. In his view, Shakespeare's 'mirror held up to nature' was rather like 'a looking glass exposed for sale, which reflects alternately the funeral and the puppet-show, the venerable beggar soliciting charity, and the rascal picking a pocket'.[10] To modern readers this may sound like a tribute to the all-embracing diversity of Shakespearean drama, but to Steevens, the violation of decorum was unforgivable. Francis Gentleman was worried by the fact that Hamlet, who was supposed to be 'a virtuous prince and a feeling man', occasionally forgot himself and behaved like a base villain.[11] Meaning to lend Shakespeare a helping hand, Gentleman suggested an alternative ending that makes his family name appear singularly appropriate:

> After the detection of the play, if his majesty, upon the principle of self-defence, had formed a design of taking the prince off by instruments at home; if that design had been made known to the Queen; had she, through maternal affection, put Hamlet on his guard; and had that prince taken measures worthy the motive of stimulation, a tyrant of some consequence and uniformity would have been shown in Claudius; a tender mother in the Queen, and a hero in Hamlet; the innocent characters, Polonius and Ophelia, might have been saved; and death prevented from stalking without limitation at the catastrophe.[12]

After such creativity, Garrick's changes seem almost protective of Shakespeare.

In 1783 John Philip Kemble's Hamlet discarded many of Davenant's minor 'improvements' from the previous century. 'Self-murder' again became 'self-slaughter', 'might not beteem' replaced Davenant's 'permitted not', and Kemble also brought back lines that had been removed in 1661: 'A beast that wants discourse of reason would have mourned longer' and 'o, most wicked speed: to post with such dexterity to incestuous sheets' (I.2). However, much still remained to be done.

On 26 November 1864 – less than five months before his brother achieved greater fame by assassinating President Lincoln in Ford's Theatre – the American Hamlet, Edwin Booth, restored the irreverent epithets addressed to the Ghost in I.5 ('truepenny', 'boy', 'old mole' and 'the fellow in the cellarage), none of which had been uttered since Burbage. Booth's loyalty to the original text did not pass unpunished. The *New York World* felt that the actor abased himself by returning to the Bard and argued that Hamlet's banter was incongruent with 'the ineffable tenderness with which he has just addressed the dread visitant'. Consistent with his friendly Hamlet, Booth hurried to excuse himself on the grounds that he meant no disrespect to the Ghost – he merely intended to portray 'the very intensity of mental excitement'. His reply admirably exemplifies how Shakespeare's text may be ignored even after it has been restored to performance. By and large Booth depended on Goethe's description of Hamlet as a 'beautiful, pure, noble, and most moral nature' that 'sinks beneath a burden which it can neither bear nor throw off'.[13]

What must be thrown off in such a portrayal of the Prince, however, are the rough treatment of Ophelia in the Nunnery scene (III.1), the lewd remarks addressed to her in the Play scene (III.2), and Hamlet's harshness towards Gertrude in the Closet scene (III.4). Even the unkind words addressed to Rosencrantz and Guildenstern in the 'Sponge speech' (IV.2) were considered out of character for Booth's gentle Dane. Still, Booth's courage should be commended for bringing back 'Now might I do it pat' (III.3) in which Hamlet primitively resolves that the mere killing of his uncle will not satisfy him. These barbaric words had been abandoned by Garrick, possibly because Dr. Johnson found the speech too horrible to be read or to be uttered.[14] However, Booth's motivation for including the speech was not to show Hamlet's fierceness, but rather to emphasize his leniency – after all, as Booth reminded us, Hamlet does not act on his words. It hardly needs mention that 'How all occasions do inform against me', in which Hamlet decides to become a merciless killer, would never fit into the Booth version and was once again cut.

In 1874, Henry Irving's contribution to the restoration of Shakespeare's *Hamlet* consisted of the '*Denmark is a prison*' dialogue from *Folio*, II.2, and in 1897, Irving's protégé Johnston Forbes Robertson took pity on Fortinbras who had been waiting in the wings for two centuries. However, the belated arrival of the Norwegian Prince did not meet with the approval of the *London World*, which found Shakespeare's original ending to be 'of no literary value'. In ridiculing the *London World* review, George Bernard Shaw wrote:

> The Forbes Robertson Hamlet at the Lyceum is, very unexpectedly at that address, really not at all unlike Shakespeare's play of the same name. I am quite certain

I saw Reynaldo in it for a moment; and possibly I may have seen Voltimand and Cornelius; but just as the time for their scene arrived, my eye fell on the word 'Fortinbras' in the program, which so amazed me that I hardly know what I saw for the next ten minutes. Ophelia, instead of being a strenuously earnest and self-possessed young lady giving a concert and recitation for all she was worth, was mad – actually mad. The story of the play was perfectly intelligible, and quite took the attention of the audience off the principal actor at moments. What is the Lyceum coming to?[15]

Nevertheless, Forbes Robertson introduced a fallacy which echoed the Romantics and was to be accepted as a legitimate interpretation for decades to come. Ignoring the testimony of the Gravedigger in V.2, his Hamlet remained on the young side of 25, with Gertrude and Claudius in their early forties.[16] Moreover, he offered a suave gentleman Hamlet in the vein of Booth and Goethe and, as others had discovered before him, such a Hamlet cannot be allowed to utter all of Shakespeare's dialogue. Hamlet's horrible 'Now might I do it pat' was once again scrapped.

When we get to 1922, the American John Barrymore delivered what Alexander Wolcott hailed as 'the realest Hamlet we have known'. Barrymore endeavoured to portray a young intellectual recognizable to a 20th century audience, and strove to be macho as well as modern, or, in his own words: 'so male that when I come out on the stage they can hear my balls clank'.[17] Barrymore foolhardily invited George Bernard Shaw to his London premiere. In the opening lines of Shaw's letter in response the perpetual curmudgeon deigned to praise Barrymore's originality, but went on to lament the fact that the production had 'cut the play to ribbons' and then filled it up with interpolated drama in the form of dumb show. Shaw made it very clear that by 'dumb' he did not only mean 'mute'.[18]

So far we have examined cuts and alterations made in order to render the hero of *Hamlet* more heroic. Since Betterton it has been a custom to confuse Hamlet with a tragically unflawed matinee idol, and, as mentioned, such a portrayal of the Prince necessitates systematic cuts in Shakespeare's text. If we wonder how generations of actors could perpetuate a tradition so obviously at odds with the actual play, part of the explanation must be that received traditions have focused on the artistic presentation rather than on the material presented. This has caused *Hamlet* to appear as a dramatic monologue with the Prince as the prima donna and all the other characters as mere supernumeraries. What Hamlet actually says has been upstaged by the way in which he says it. In a typical review from 1922 we see several Hamlets compared in a way that suggests opera rather than drama:

Mounet-Sully's Hamlet was richer and more sonorous, Forbes-Robertson's at times more sublimated; Irving's more sharply devised; and Sothern's, so far as we are concerned with the verse pattern, was more securely read.[19]

In the television programme *Shakespeare's Women* Claire Bloom informs us that the 'proper way' to speak Shakespeare until the middle of the 20th century was to *recite* it, like a musical score. Claire Bloom produces in evidence a sample of a 1929 voice coaching, as performed by Mrs. Patrick Campbell who stresses the 'fundamental and supreme value of beautiful speech' in the art of acting. While frantically wringing her hands, Mrs. Campbell delivers snippets of Lady Macbeth's sleepwalking scene in a way that would evacuate a modern theatre in seconds: (*in a deep, autumnal tone*) 'Ah-a-a-out ... dam-ned spot ... Out I (*scaling up and down*) SAY-yeh! (*in a pitched voice*): Yet, who'd have thought ...(*chanting*) the o-o-old man-n-n-n ... to have had-uh ... so much bah-lud in him-m-m-m-uh?'

In 1937, Granville Barker wrote:

> The production of the plays is thus still apt to be marked by a timid respect for 'the usual thing'; their acting is crippled by pseudo-traditions, which are inert because they are not Shakespearean at all. They are the accumulation of two centuries of progressive misconception and distortion of the playwright's art.[20]

It stands to reason that spectators and actors submerged in detailed intonation studies must inevitably lose sight of the play as a whole. When Frank Benson presented the first complete *Hamlet* in the summer of 1899,[21] no one seemed to notice how the full text radically changed the traditional view of the hero. Thirty-five years later, however, when John Gielgud took on *Hamlet* in its entirety (or, as some actors said, 'its eternity')[22] he did not fail to realize that the text revealed a particularly churlish Hamlet:

> There are so many unpleasant things in this man's character and in the part of Hamlet. The actors in all the traditional performances rather sweeten them. I read how Tree had come back in the Nunnery scene and kissed Ophelia's hair behind her back .... The part had been so romanticized, and Goethe had said that Hamlet was a precious Grecian urn broken by the flowers or something very, very sententious, and all the kind of coarse and lively thrust of the play came upon me when we did it at the Vic. (...) I thought that too much beauty was perhaps not a good thing, and I kept on trying, whenever I played Hamlet, to find the bad sides.[23]

It would seem, however, that Gielgud did not look hard enough for bad sides in the character, but, inadvertently or otherwise, clung to a score of romantic accretions, such as Hamlet's undoubted love for his father and for Ophelia, together with a rather lofty acting voice. When Gielgud played the part again in 1944, the *Spectator* dismissed his performance as 'mere eloquence, admirable academic eloquence'.[24]

We might have expected the world finally to be ready for '*Hamlet* as Shakespeare meant it' by the 1950s. The theatre had abandoned most of its received, fustian traditions, and what Granville Barker referred to as the 'pornographic difficulty' – the bawdy jokes still not permitted in the 1930s – had been cleared away, although Eric Partridge had explained all the jokes in 1947. But, alas, Shakespeare was instead ushered into the Theatre of the Absurd and on to Postmodernism.

In 1982, James Fenton jibed: 'For a masterpiece to come alive to us, and for it to come alive continually, it must be made strange. This is the generally given and accepted notion of theatrical aesthetics'.[25] Made for the sole purpose of confusing the audience, it seems, is Coronada's film from 1976, with a set of naked twins playing Hamlet (Anthony and David Meyer), and with both Ophelia and Gertrude played by Helen Mirren (if Hamlet cannot tell the two women apart in the Nunnery scene III.1, why should we?). In 1979, at a time when the world believed that Germany was pacified after two world wars and would not bother anyone again, Heiner Müller launched his *Hamletmaschine*, a postmodern massacre of Shakespeare's play, traces of which could be seen at Kronborg Castle as late as in the summer of 2004 (do I mean traces of Müller or traces of Shakespeare? The answer is: both). Almereyda's film version (2000) was set in the Manhattan world of finance, and Jasenko Selimovich's Swedish production from the 1990s took us to the battlefields of Kosovo, evidently on the assumption that the audience would be unable on their own to draw a parallel between Fortinbras' Polish campaign and the wars that still go on today. Such allusions to modern-day life are what Jan Kott termed 'forced topicality'[26], and Jonathan Miller elaborates: 'the text becomes an occasion for something else; it's a pretext rather than a text'.[27]

However, partly justifying forced topicality are the overly 'true to tradition' productions described by James Fenton:

> The difficulty in directing *Hamlet* in England today is to prevent that irritating sense of anticipation in the audience, which can sometimes be heard – like the electronic pre-echo on a malfunctioning record-player – as each received interpretation clicks into place. Imagine an experience of *Hamlet* which was no more than a reliving of one's A-level years – a fearful thought, and yet not perhaps an untypical experience of the play.[28]

In view of such 'when-I-ope-my-lips-let-no-dog-bark' productions in which High Priests of Bardolatry take it all much more seriously than Shakespeare ever did, it is hardly odd that stage people occasionally feel obliged to treat this Leviathan of a tragedy to a new and radical approach. Crazy things done to *Hamlet* are not confined to modern times. When Samuel Pepys saw the play back in 1663, he was disappointed that his wife's maid Gosnell, who had been given a minor part, neither sang nor danced – from which we may infer that the 1663 production of *Hamlet* had been turned into a musical extravaganza. In 1793, a theatre bill from the *Kilkenny Theatre Royal* read:

> The Tragedy of *Hamlet*. Originally written and composed by the celebrated Dan. Hayes of Limerick, and inserted in Shakespeare's works. Hamlet by Mr. Kearns, (being his first appearance in that character) who, between the acts, will perform several solos on the patent bagpipes, which play two tunes at the same time. Ophelia by Mrs. Prior, who will introduce several favourite airs in character, particularly "The Lass of Richmond Hill" and "We'll all be unhappy together", from the reverend Mr. Dibdin's oddities.[29]

It is hard to see how Richmond Hill may fit in, but Dibdin's last oddity seems written for the occasion. Nineteenth-century America matched such antics with deliberate travesties:

> Audiences roared at the sight of Hamlet dressed in fur cap and collar, snowshoes and mittens; they listened with amused surprise to his profanity when ordered by his father's ghost to 'swear' .... [30]

The early nineteenth century offered a 'canine Hamlet' in which a trained dog followed Hamlet throughout five acts until it eventually assisted its master in killing the guilty King.[31]

After such clear instances of comic relief, we may return to Shaw's issue of *Hamlet* 'as Shakespeare meant it', and must conclude that for many an actor or director working within the conventions of his particular period, the Danish Prince has proved too complex a character. More than a handful of Hamlets have short-changed us with substantial trimmings of the text in order to alter the image of the Dane from what he was into something rather more heroic and acceptable. As we have seen, the theatre is not solely to blame. Occasional reversions to the original text have caused critics to censure Shakespeare for coarseness, and academics attempting to distort Shakespeare are still at large. However, if Shakespeare's criticism of his protagonist is removed from *Hamlet* – as has been done for centuries – we have no choice but to assume that the author sanctions the murder of three innocent people, or, if we want to avoid that, no choice but to perform character assassination on Polonius, Rosencrantz and Guildenstern in order to justify Hamlet's actions. The efforts to turn Hamlet into a romantic hero – and every season has sent forth a new one, be it a Werther, a Gavrilo Princip, or a James Dean – have all quite disregarded the fact that Shakespeare's text describes the Royal Dane not only as a victim of circumstance, but also as callous, self-centred, pesky and brutal. Directors, actors and critics in search of a hero have also ignored one of Dr. Johnson's most lucid observations on Shakespeare, although it has been plain for all to read since 1765:

> Shakespeare has no heroes; his scenes are occupied only by men, who act and think as the reader thinks that he should have spoken or acted on the same occasion.[32]

On his visit to London in 1775, the German scientist Georg Cristoph Lichtenberg wittily observed that in England, Shakespeare was 'not only famous, but holy',[33] and that 'To be or not to be' had been elevated almost to the level of the Lord's Prayer. Even so, divinity is often treated with alarming disobedience and, like crusaders going to battle and butchery in order to propagate the Christian message of brotherly love, bardolators frequently forget their own prophet in the process of producing his plays. It would seem that the miracle of Shakespeare is not that he has remained popular for 400 years, but rather that he has survived four centuries of liberal constructions and alterations of his plays, and of *Hamlet* more than any other. Behind all efforts to save Shakespeare or spare the spectators lurks the *Hamlet* that Shakespeare wrote. I believe we are still waiting to see it hit the stage or the screen.

Notes

[1] George Bernard Shaw, *Shaw on Shakespeare*, Letter of 27 July, 1897. p. 101
[2] E.K. Chambers, *Shakespearean Gleanings*, p. 40
[3] Samuel Schoenbaum, *Shakespeare, A Compact Documentary Life*, pp. 224-227 and Stephen Greenblatt, *Will in the World*, p. 331
[4] Bernard Grebanier, *Then Came Each Actor*, p. 114.
[5] *New Variorum II*, p. 157
[6] John A. Mills, *Hamlet on Stage, The Great Tradition*, p. 27
[7] *New Variorum II*, pp. 244-245
[8] Carol Jones Carlisle, *Shakespeare from the Greenroom*, p. 36
[9] *The Cambridge History of English and American Literature*, Vol. XI, XV, § 5.
[10] Carlisle, p. 36

11 Ibid. p. 38
12 Ibid. p. 40
13 Goethe, *Wilhelm Meister*, quoted in *New Variorum II*, p. 273
14 *New Variorum I*, p. 283
15 Shaw, pp. 101-102
16 Mills, p. 176
17 Ibid. p. 191
18 From Stark Young's review of Barrymore's Hamlet, The New Republican, 6 December, 1922
19 Granville Barker, Preface to Hamlet (1937), Nick Hern Books (2003), p. 3
20 Shaw, pp. 95-97
21 Grebanier, p. 421
22 Mills, p. 209
23 Transcribed from the 1978 broadcast *An Actor and his Time*, in which Gielgud was interviewed by John Miller.
24 Mills, p. 226
25 Fenton: *Times Literary Supplement*, September 17, 1982
26 Jan Kott, *Shakespeare Our Contemporary*, p. 48
27 Hastrup, p. 159
28 Fenton, *Times Literary Supplement*, September 17, 1982
29 Grebanier, p. 263
30 Lawrence L. Levine, *Highbrow, Lowbrow*, pp. 13-14
31 Grebanier, p. 263
32 Samuel Johnson, *Preface to Shakespeare's Plays*, p. xi
33 Mills, p. 40

WORKS CITED

Barker, Harley Granville, *Preface to Hamlet* (1937) (London: Nick Hern Books, 1993)

Carlisle, Carol Jones, *Shakespeare from the Greenroom* (Chapel Hill, University of North Carolina Press, 1969)

Chambers, E.K., *Shakespearean Gleanings* (London: Oxford University Press, 1944)

Fenton, James, 'In the Study and on the Stage' (in *Times Literary Supplement*, September 17, 1982).

Furness, Horace Howard, *Hamlet: New Variorum Edition II* (New York: Dover Publications, 1963).

Grebanier, Bernard, *Then Came Each Actor* (New York: McKay, 1975).

Greenblatt, Stephen, *Will in the World* (London: Jonathan Cape, 2004).

Hastrup, Kirsten, *Action: Anthropology in the Company of Shakespeare* (Copenhagen: Museum Tusculanum Press, 2004).

Johnson, Samuel, *Preface to Shakespeare's Plays* (Menston, U.K.: Scolar, 1969).

Kott, Jan, *Shakespeare Our Contemporary*, (London: Methuen, 1965).

Levine, Lawrence L., *Highbrow, Lowbrow*, (Cambridge, Massachusetts: Harvard University Press, 1988).

Mills, John A., *Hamlet on Stage: The Great Tradition* (London: Greenwood Press, 1985).

Schoenbaum, Samuel, *Shakespeare A Compact Documentary Life* (New York: Oxford University Press, 1977)

Shaw, George Bernard, *Shaw on Shakespeare*, ed. Edwin Wilson (New York: E.P. Dutton, 1961)

HAMLET AND THE PLAYERS:
PERFORMANCE AND APPROPRIATION OF SHAKESPEARE IN EAST BERLIN

Robert Weimann

Since in our time the reception of Shakespeare is a 'world phenomenon,' we should be wary of supposing there can be any master clue for coming to terms with the dramatist's texts on modern stages. Rather, there is good reason, as Christy Desmet warns us, to challenge two concepts of appropriation which have all too easily been entertained in the recent past: one is 'the idea that Shakespeare must always already be co-opted by the dominant culture'; the other is 'the easy assumption that Shakespeare can set us free.'[1] In other words, a critical assessment of Shakespeare's treatment on modern stages is well advised to use the concept of 'appropriation' only with certain qualifications. As a 'world phenomenon' (again, Desmet's phrase) Shakespeare is nobody's property; to appropriate his work for the stage is at best an act of cultural assimilation which is demanding in more than one way. First of all, the bard's remains, in whichever form, demand respect; as Michael Bristol notes, any literary value makes sense only on the condition 'that the economy of literary works is seen in terms of gifts rather than of commodities.' And as gifts, 'great literary works entail particularly complex and onerous obligations.'[2]

If, with these provisions in mind, I adopt the concept of 'appropriation,' I am using it in the non-acquisitive and non-juridical sense of *Aneignung*, of intellectually, mentally as well as materially, as through its performance, making the work one's own. The political economy of the gift stipulates reciprocity. In other words, *Aneignung* connotes more than *taking* a cultural work instrumentally for one's own purposes only; it is not good enough to use the text as a ground on which to flaunt directorial originality or as a means of easy audience satisfaction. Rather, the obligation is to *give* the work our own, our best, most thoughtful and most tactful response to what impulses and resistances we confront when, legitimately, re-reading a play fruitfully, as in close contact with our own changing world.

To introduce these questions of method and approach may be particularly appropriate when, as in the present essay, the politics of Shakespearean appropriation looms as large as in most theatrical productions of Shakespeare in the European countries of the former Soviet Bloc. In view of a rather heavy burden of ideology informing premises and expectations at the time, but even perhaps among today's readers, it may appear only fair and reasonable for me briefly to articulate my own historicizing perspective. As I see it, there are two kinds of approaches that do not appear to be helpful. The first of these is one that essentially pursues a salvaging operation. There is no point, I believe, in taking a defensive or nostalgic stance, or even attempting to rescue certain aims and positions in a Shakespeare reception that, arguably, has in the past been used to resist basic cultural trends in an age of irresistible change and conflict. The second type of approach that appears to me to be equally unhelpful is that which, focusing purely on past contradictions and liabilities, pursues the all too predictable conclusion that Shakespeare's reception 'under Communism' was an altogether deplorable aberration from the true standards of Western culture. Rejecting both these salvaging and muckraking operations, I propose to plead for a less predictable approach. According to this approach, a set of highly diverse and contradictory discourses so happened to intersect in and through the East and Central European reception of Shakespeare, that the latter allowed for both unsuspected openings and orthodox closures in the criticism and production, in Eastern Europe, of potentially the greatest cultural text of modern Western civilization. What we had was, then, an encounter of discourses, marked by a good deal of incompatibility and instability, a site of political and cultural circumstances on which the reception of Shakespeare constituted discursive practices through which profound social and intellectual contradictions of the time were intercepted, assimilated or displaced.

Such appropriation of a Western classic must not of course be thought of as anything homogeneous; nor should important differences in the cultural scenario among the countries involved be overlooked. Even within each of the East and Central European countries, the appropriation of Shakespeare took varying forms; the performance of his plays in the theatre was discontinuous rather than otherwise from what the academic criticism of Shakespeare endeavored to do. All these levels of difference must not be minimized, even though, I shall argue, it was precisely at the point of intersection between theatrical and critical discourses that the more illuminating insights and tensions in the assimilation of the classic emerged.

Along these lines, the appropriation of Shakespeare in East Germany pursued a specific cultural and intertextual focus. In fact, it may well be said that the performance of his plays was particularly rewarding where their production was (dis)continuous with critical trends in contemporary scholarship. As far as I can judge from my own experience, the cooperation between scholarship and theatrical practice at the time could be productive but it was also problematic and ambivalent. It is true, dialogue and cooperation were officially encouraged. But the response to such encouragement was far from being a totally controllable gesture. While on the one hand the Shakespeare scholar was officially expected to assist the actors and, if necessary, to tell them which reading of the text was the politically correct one, it was, on the other hand, possible to circumvent this presumptuous, arrogant expectation. Thus, the role of the consultant was not an entirely predictable one. To work with theatre people through a lengthy period of rehearsals had a dynamic all of its own, one that could never quite be reduced to the ideology of any preconceived notion of the play's given or desirable meaning.

Even so, it was difficult for a consultant entirely to extricate herself/himself from what was then considered to be the social function of the theatre. But what politics such function implied and what kind of political awareness resulted was a question beset by a good deal of ambivalence. Therefore, here to recall the role of the theatre in state-administered socialist societies can be entirely misleading unless a critical distinction is observed between the dominant political definition and prescription of this social function and the way the theatre actually played it out. Obviously, the two were never the same, because even when the theatre's management and its own publicized project were completely marked by orthodoxy, the result – that is, the performed play – inevitably was exposed to multivocal mediation and response through the work of actors interacting with not quite predictable occasions and audiences. In a situation like this the East German theatre more often than not tended to play out a type of cultural politics characterized by a desire to discover something new within and beyond the dominating Marxist analysis of history, something that often enough was marked by complicity with unorthodox audience perceptions and expectations. In these circumstances, it was not surprising that audiences, as Lawrence Guntner pointedly notes, came 'to expect, and party cultural functionaries came to suspect, that Shakespeare productions might just (and often did) contain gift-wrapped critiques of the East German version of the Socialist system'.[3] Fully to appreciate these audience expectations, we need to remember that, since a freely accessible, open public sphere did not for all practical purposes exist, the stage came to assume the role of a public forum where cultural ideology and, by extension, the socialist claims and problems of the state could be staged, debated, but also intercepted and criticized. Newspapers, television, radio, and books could be and were censored in the sense that they constituted media which were directly controlled, even partially processed by the authorities. But there was no official theatre censorship office as such; in East Germany, for example, only the year's repertory had to be submitted to the *Direktion für Bühnenrepertoire* for approval.

Thus, paradoxically, the cultural reception of the classic made it possible that the state-administered uses of ideology behind the closure of representation could be radically questioned. Let me, at this point, introduce as an illustration the production of *Hamlet* directed by Benno Besson, at the Berlin Volksbühne in 1977. This production, for which, following the director's invitation, I was privileged to serve as consultant,[4] pursued several of the readings that I had first explored in the German version (1967) of my study, *Shakespeare and the Popular Tradition in the Theater*; at the same time, there may well have been memories of Adolf Dresen's and Maik Hamburger's legendary Greifswald production of *Hamlet* in 1964. But Besson's *Hamlet*, more than a decade later, reached further in at least one direction when it went out of its way to emphasize a deep rift between neoclassical order in the humanist poetics of the Prince of Denmark and the sheer expertise, competence and experience of the players. Rather than minimizing these tensions in the language of the play, Besson's version of *Hamlet* surrendered any univocal assertion of 'the purpose of playing' in favor of a more complex projection of a divided space for socio-cultural representation.

Thus, Besson's production, using Heiner Müller's adaptation of Maik Hamburger's Greifswald translation of the play, in no uncertain terms challenged the adequacy of neoclassical-romantic standards of appropriating Shakespeare's text for the modern stage. Rejecting any purely humanist reading of the role of the Prince of Denmark, the production emphasized instead the 'muddy-mettled rascal,' the 'John-a-dreams,' who could refer to himself as 'a rogue and peasant slave' (II, ii, 502-20). The idea was not to play down the Elizabethan mingle-mangle, where 'the toe of the peasant comes so near the heel of the courtier' (V, i, 136-7), but to redefine a mobile social relationship that appeared to affect the circulation of authority inside the theatre itself.

In this context, Besson – generally recognized as the most talented and internationally influential director among Brecht's disciples – contributed a striking rereading of Hamlet's advice to the players that, in our present context, deserves especially to be considered. As, I suppose, was the case in most European countries, Hamlet's advice to the players was a canonized text on which generations of actors were brought up and led to believe in that classical 'smoothness' and balance in the interplay between performed 'action' and written 'word' (III, ii, 17-9). As the famous phrase goes, 'Suit the action to the word, the word to the action, with this special observance, that you o'erstep not the modesty of nature.' This indeed was sound advice, except that, upon scrutiny, what appears a cogent and altogether impartial pronouncement is couched in the context of a not at all unbiased character. The bias manifests itself in the strong emphasis on a certain 'purpose of playing' which is defined in that its 'end, both at the first and now, was and is to hold as `twere the mirror up to nature.' Continuity between times past and time present is called upon to fortify time-honoured classical learning as an incontrovertible site of authority. To corroborate this type of authority, Hamlet invokes the 'judicious,'[5] those, let it be remembered, who can worship a play that 'was never acted,' that 'pleased not the million' and was 'caviare to the general' (II , ii, 430-3), and whose 'censure' was assumed to have weight enough that 'must in your allowance o'erweigh a whole theatre of others' (III, ii, 28).

In East German cultural politics, this neoclassical definition of 'the purpose of playing' was especially canonical in that it was used in every cultural and theatrical school and institution as the fountain-head of dramatic realism. How shocking, then, for Besson to present in this scene an obtrusive, loquacious Prince – acted by Manfred Karge – who delivered his platitudes with an air of self-conceit inseparable from the pompous enunciation of these all-too familiar principles. No less striking was the stance of the First Player. As he was told to 'Speak the speech, I pray you, as I pronounced it to you, trippingly on the tongue'(III, ii, 1-2), the First Player's response conveyed through facial and gestural expression was that of an impatient skeptic: here, obviously, was a practitioner, slightly bored by mere theory, who appeared to know more about histrionic delivery than any theoretical disquisition could teach him. Suffering the self-conceited fool of a princely Maecenas gladly, the player went through the motions, clearly understating social distance with his 'I warrant your honour,' and a rather proud and none too polite 'I hope we have reformed that indifferently with us' (36).

The remarkable thing was that this reading could be so sustained in the production, that, convincingly, it appeared to be a variation of what elsewhere in the play emerged as a location of conflict between text and performance. Thus, the scene harkened back to the well publicized tension between child actors and writers in the private theatres, as when Rosencrantz reports that 'the poet and the player went to cuffs in the question' (II, ii, 354). Although there was, of course, no open conflict when the author of 'a speech of some dozen or sixteen lines' (II, v, 535) presumed to advise the performer in his own craft, yet Besson's reading provided Hamlet's lengthy advice with the dramatic thrust of a substantial conflict. Challenging not simply the poetic validity of the neoclassical doctrine of *imitatio vitae*, this reading defied the privileged status and education of the Prince of Denmark and, with it, a strictly literate authority, one predicated on a humanistic belief in the dignity and stability of the text itself.

This reinterpretation of Hamlet's famous advice to the players—far from being a mere gimmick—drew attention to what was a cultural division of discourses and authorities in the Elizabethan theatre. On the one hand, there was the discourse of humanism and neo-Aristotelian representation, the masterful uses of a mode of imitation that involved a 'conquest of the world as picture,' establishing the measure for everything and, thereby, affirming, in Heidegger's phrase, 'unlimited power for the calculating, planning, and molding of all things'.[6] It is against this discourse of representation that the performer and the performative thrust of Hamlet's madness itself provided a counterpoint. Besson's interpretation provided us with a corrective agency of considerable resilience, when it was suggested that 'holding the mirror up to nature' was not good enough, even though it did of course sanction the strong self-representation of the courtier's, soldier's, scholar's image in the play. Accordingly, there was a sense of forces inside the play resisting any single masterful code of representation, jeopardizing it through antic clowning, disguise, 'ecstasy,' and other audience-related forms of performative practice.

To learn from Besson's theatre was to scrutinize the text of Hamlet's advice more critically. Could it be that Hamlet's language itself invited a divisive response? Was it possible that Shakespeare the actor wrote with tongue in cheek when referring to Hamlet's own pronouncing the speech as 'trippingly on the tongue'? 'Trippingly' could be read as 'in a nimble, light-footed manner;' but 'tripping' is also what Kent in his disguise does to Oswald so as to make him stumble or what Hermione says to Polixenes, 'you have tripp'd since.' (I,i,76). Hence, as the OED records, 'tripping' in this sense is 'stumbling,' especially 'to stumble in articulation; to falter in speaking' ('trip,' under v. 8. b.). Here, there was at least the possibility that, thanks to a careful rereading of Shakespeare's potential meanings, the production itself culminated in a contrarious play on words. And Hamlet, as we know, uses wordplay far more profusely than any other Shakespearean character: M.M. Mahood in her study of *Shakespeare's Wordplay* counted almost ninety puns.

Besson's *Hamlet* had a remarkable impact on the East German cultural scene. Hamlet, the presumed representative of both humanism and the people, was effectively (and without much fuss) dislodged from his former pre-eminence as premature harbinger of idealized news about a revolutionary future. Here, indeed, a canonized tradition was practically questioned in terms of both what (in Shakespeare's text) was represented and what (in the contemporary theatre) was doing the presenting and performing. Basic presuppositions of authority and validity, hitherto governing selection and control over a given canon, had ceased to be operative. As was the case in Greifswald in 1964, the theatre itself challenged the politics of canonization through which the alleged certainties in a masterful use of the past were designed to control and contain whatever uncertainty the future held.

The question, then, needed to be confronted whether there was an alternative to an understanding of the Shakespearean *Erbe*, or heritage, that, arrogantly, claimed to institute a possessive, totalizing, self-congratulatory mode of ownership over texts and discourses of the past. Was it perhaps possible, on the strength of the performative element in the theatre, to undermine the canonized uses of Shakespeare? And to do that in such a way that the reception in the present of his plays would *not* have to be regarded as an illusory project by which some ideological consciousness (or reason, in its presumed autonomy) hoped to extend its sense of sovereignty and continuity to the events and figures of the past? As far as these questions did receive an affirmative answer, there emerged in Besson's production a site on which the textual meaning of representation and the energies of performance could mutually engage one another. Such engagement was highly consequential in that it helped constitute a thoroughly viable space for revitalizing the classic in the ever changeful world of its reception. Over and beyond a mutually significant 'interference' between then and now, there unfolded in performance a discursive practice in which textual authority—far from being given—could re-inaugurate itself as part of a larger circulation of cultural agencies in playful rehearsal.

It was in response to this perspective that, I felt, the popular tradition in the Elizabethan theatre deserved to be further studied and adapted to the modern stage. Clearly, this tradition could not adequately be dealt with in terms of the nineteenth-century concept of *narodnostj*, let alone by its Marxist-Leninist redefinition that presupposed humanist standards as mediated by Enlightenment rationality. Instead, it seemed more promising to reopen the debate on more recent grounds, such as those developed in the path-breaking approaches of S. L. Bethell and C. L. Barber, or by Terence Hawkes' eye-opening study of Shakespeare's *Talking Animals: Language in Drama and Society*. At the same time, what was needed was a new emphasis and focus on the incommensurate quality of a performative practice that could never quite be subsumed under any exclusive uses of textual meaning. In this respect, the study of the popular tradition in the theatre opened up a challenging potential both on the Shakespearean stage and in our reception of his plays. That stage, as I had suggested, did not contain any unified type of theatrical space; there was a disparity between the symbolically charged locus as textually prescribed site of what meaning was represented as in a fiction, and the partially nonsymbolic platea (as a site of what actually was materially there, visibly, audibly performing on the platform stage). This disparity, of central importance to Shakespeare's stage, precluded the self-contained autonomy of any textually prescribed role. On the contrary, on this stage role and actor, textual authority and performative agency would enter into a relationship that, spatially, socially, and semiotically, was an open one, offering space for both continuity and discontinuity between these two dimensions.

If this was so, the reproduction of Shakespeare's plays in our time was ill-advised to favor a unitary concept of theatrical space that by itself would compel a univocally fixed mode in the relations of scriptural and nonscriptural signs and meanings. As against such closure of theatrical space, the Shakespearean text appeared to me to be most congenial to a modern appropriation wherever the stage was conceived to be both 'individable' and dividable. Such flexibly staged scene would offer space for signifying practices which contradict and answer one another and which decline to annihilate themselves in a final global meaning. In the East German reception of Shakespeare, this aperture was rarely achieved, despite considerable attention bestowed on plebeian characters. Brecht after all was well-advised when he said that today Shakespeare's plays can best be revitalized when first of all his theatre is revisited in the context of its own circumstantial history.

Brecht's warning itself must be seen against the background of Shakespeare's eighteenth- and early nineteenth-century reception and the formation of a *Nationaltheater* that Lessing and others had called for. As Maik Hamburger has pointed out, Brecht's own theatrical project with its emphasis on *gestus*, on the gestic and performative qualities of drama, was in critical response to the purely literary orientation of an earlier middle-class theatre culture. As opposed to Shakespeare's own proximity to all kinds of popular, colloquial, oral speech and corporeal action, that middle-class culture tended to deepen a deplorable 'gulf between literary language and everyday speech.' It did so by cutting the link between highly literary translations of the Bard and the dramatic uses of the language of 'popular speech' and 'everyday life'.[7]

Thus, to shift the emphasis somewhat, on the stage of the European Enlightenment, the authority of dramatic language as a source of moral sensibility and the refinement of social and emotional relations reigned supreme. But that, precisely, was the language of an educated poet-dramatist whose precept was invoked, in Friedrich Ludwig Schröder's words, as an entirely binding *Vorschrift des Dichters,* as, literally, the 'prescription of the poet,' that is, as a thoroughly prescribed authority. But what has less often been noticed is that such textual authority was theatrically used to ensure unity between performer and performed. The notion of textual authority sanctioned by the 'aims' or 'intentions' of the poet invariably went hand in hand with the attempt to proscribe any gap between the impersonator and the impersonated. In other words, the call for the authority of the dramatist over the work of the performer was not an innocent gesture. This gesture culminated in the closure of representation. To close the gap between what was representing and what was represented was one way of keeping out uncomfortable elements, such as 'that low stuff' in the productions of Shakespeare (to echo Sir Thomas Hanmer's Preface to his 1711 edition of Shakespeare).[8] If, then, in several European countries the appropriation of his plays could assume the status almost of a national shrine, that shrine served as a monumental and yet highly partial medium of inspiration. Although widely celebrated as universally valid, the reception of that heritage was, even at the height of nineteenth-century bardolatry, an exclusive one. Rather than being, as postulated, all-inclusive, it sought to preserve inviolate the literary art of the poet vis-à-vis the irreverent zest, the game, the craft and craftiness of the performer.

As this critical excursion into the history of a predominantly literary reception of Shakespeare suggests, the interrelationship in the theatre between textually inscribed meanings and the strategies of performative practice was always already marked by a cultural politics of a sort. As today we look back upon the underlying uses of both cultural difference and confederation in the Elizabethan public theatres, it is difficult not to be struck by mid-twentieth-century analogies or, even, continuities in the circulation of a specifically scriptural authority in modern Shakespeare productions. Ironically, yet not quite unexpectedly, an antihistrionic (though not an antitheatrical) prejudice was resurrected almost wholesale, on a programmatic level, in some of the socialist countries in post-war Eastern Europe, but especially so in East Germany. Here, the dominant politics of reception sought to invoke authoritative precedent and, of course, legitimization in reference to the privileged emphasis on the written word in the formative period of the nation's cultural history. Accordingly, the emphasis was on the authority of the classical text as best compatible with realism in the theatre à la Stanislavsky. Together, these influential constellations culminated in the strategies of empathy and closure. At its centre, there was a poetics that, without much ado, equated a Renaissance concept of 'nature' with 'society,' so as to postulate a traditionally sanctioned platform for realism. For that, Hamlet's advice to the players, 'to hold as 'twere the mirror up to nature,' was assumed to be at the heart of both Shakespeare's credo and our own credentials for a competent reception of his work.

It was at this point that, finally, the reception of poststructuralism served as a very welcome leaven permeating critical thought and international discussion in the East German Shakespeare Society.[9] There, the emerging focus on discourse, power, authority, and representation in terms of Shakespeare's textual and theatrical practices, initiated during the Weimar Society conference of 1983, was a surprisingly unorthodox move; most likely, it was among the earliest, if it was not the first, of such attempts in Germany to assimilate as well as to modify the new theoretical paradigm in terms of a sustained historical/theoretical reconsideration of a centrally canonized author. Two years later, this critical reorientation motivated and served significantly to key the agenda of the 1985 Weimar conference. It appears difficult to believe that these developments would have been feasible without having throughout the late 1970s and the 1980s a continuously fruitful dialogue with, and a point of provocative reference in, the annual performances of Shakespeare's plays.

In conclusion, therefore, the best way to summarize this brief foray is to say that the appropriation of Shakespeare in East German post-war theatre and criticism constituted a public site on which cultural communications inhabited an ambivalent space between political control and unorthodoxy, between ideological dogma and a search for a forceful, irrepressible performative. Although insignificant, of course, when measured by the larger political issues of the cold war period, the ambivalence in question was inseparable from what politics informed, or was displaced by, a remarkable encounter of discourses East and West. The theatre in particular constituted a self-challenging, conflicting location where the discourse of Marxism-Leninism, endorsed and administered by the state apparatus, was not only bound to confront the foremost Western classic but where the country's cultural politics was exposed to the risk of being challenged by this same classic. As happened in Greifswald as early as 1964 as well as in Berlin and a few other places, it was in performance and through performance that petrified doctrine, any prefigured repertoire of reception was conclusively overcome. Here, precisely, the Shakespearean play could, through its performance, constitute a certain recollection of its stagings as 'sites of popular authority.'[10] Such sites eluded political orthodoxy and the means to control public expression; and yet they thrived in a conjuncture through which the contemporary stage and the historicizing study of Shakespeare's theatre could come together in a vulnerable kind of alliance. It was an alliance that allowed for a broader awareness of the conjunctural potential residing in both the links and the gaps between then and now, between the poetic world of passions represented in the plays and our own passionate desire through performance and research to recall that world as a critical reminder of, and imaginative pointer to, what life in the present leaves to be desired.

Notes

[1] *Shakespeare and Appropriation*, eds. Christy Desmet and Robert Sawyer (London: Routledge, 1999), p.3.

[2] Michael D. Bristol, *Big-time Shakespeare* (London: Routledge, 1996), p. 144. However, while Bristol suggests that notions of 're-invention, reproduction, and appropriation describe the ensemble of responses to the market, where in the final analysis there is no recognition of obligation' (p. 146), it is possible, even within the semantics of the English word 'appropriation,' to go beyond the commercial connotation. See, e. g., Desmet (op. cit., p. 4) who notes that the term 'implies an exchange, either the theft of something valuable (such as property or ideas) or a gift, the allocation of resources for a worthy cause (such as the legislative appropriation of funds for a new school).' While the latter use of the word surely does not inform its more widely held connotations, there is some evidence for it, especially in nineteenth-century financial or foundational documents. Still, while the more frequent meaning ('the making of a thing private property,' or 'the thing ... taken possession of' (*OED*, under 1.) certainly predominates, we have a less instrumental use as early as in *The Merchant of Venice*, where Portia ironically remarks about the 'Neapolitan prince,' that 'he makes it a great appropriation, to his own good parts that he can shoe him [his horse] himself' (I, ii, 41-43). Here and in what follows, my text is *The Riverside Shakespeare*, ed. G. Blakemore Evans, 2nd edn. (Boston: Houghton Mifflin, 1997).

[3] *Redefining Shakespeare: Literary Theory and Theater Practice in the German Democratic Republic*, eds. Lawrence Guntner and Andrew M. McLean (Newark: University of Delaware Press, 1998), p. 3.

[4] My own debt to Besson's *Hamlet* is such that to this day his production of the play continues to be in my mind, even when developing further relations between 'Renaissance writing and common playing,' as in my recent *Author's Pen and Actor's Voice: Playing and Writing in Shakespeare's Theatre* (Cambridge University Press, 2000), pp. 151-179. For a long perspective on Besson's work, see my collage, 'Hamlet in Ostberlin – und kein Ende,' in *Benno Besson. Theater spielen in acht Ländern*, ed. Christa Neubert-Herwig (Berlin: Alexander Verlag, 1998), pp. 191-200.

⁵ On the 'fastidiousness' and the newness of Hamlet's use of 'judicious', see Leo Salingar, 'Jacobean playwrights and "judicious" spectators,' in *British Academy Shakespeare Lectures*, 1980-89, ed. E. A. J. Honigmann (Oxford: Oxford University Press, 1993), pp. 231-253; esp. pp. 231 f.

⁶ Martin Heidegger, 'The Age of the World Picture,' *The Question Concerning Technology and Other Essays*, trans. William Lovitt (New York: Harper and Row, 1977), pp. 115-54; cit. pp. 134 f.

⁷ Maik Hamburger, 'Gestus and the Popular Theatre,' *Science and Society*, 41 (1977), p. 41.

⁸ *Eighteenth Century Essays on Shakespeare*, ed. David Nichol Smith (New York: Russel and Russel, 1962), pp. 85-88; cit. p. 86.

⁹ I have discussed the impact of post-structuralism at greater length in an essay 'A Divided Heritage: Conflicting Appropriations of Shakespeare in (East) Germany', *Shakespeare and National Culture*, ed. by John J. Joughin (Manchester University Press, 1997), pp. 173-205.

¹⁰ Charles Whitney, 'Ante-aesthetics. Towards a Theory of Early Modern Audience Response' in *Shakespeare and Modernity. Early Modern to Millennium*, ed. Hugh Grady (London: Routledge, 2000), p. 58. Such authority was intricately linked to a variable mode of performance allowing for 'a complex alternation of audience engagement with the illusory stage world and the audience's detached awareness of the play as a play.' Ultimately, this variability inspired the Globe's motto 'Totus mundus agit histrionem,' which can be taken to stand for the idea 'that characters, players, and play-goers are all encompassed in one articulated theatrical continuum, not entirely divided into knower and known' (ibid., p. 47).

MACBETH: THE PLAY IN PERFORMANCE

Paul Edmondson

Darkness, witchcraft, and bloody daggers; spells, apparitions, and shrieks of the night owl; a drunken Porter, the ghost of a dead friend, and a bubbling cauldron; a stolen crown, the slaughter of the innocents, terrible dreams, and even the smoke of Hell itself. Whatever our impressions of *Macbeth* are, Shakespeare's drama set in eleventh-century Scotland is packed with superlative and richly resonant images that stretch way beyond the mere printed text, beyond the dialogue spoken on a stage. Poetic impressionism, however powerful, does not make great drama. The impact that Shakespeare achieves with *Macbeth* is inextricably bound up with the raw human emotions, portrayed through an intensely economic dialogue. In thinking about *Macbeth* in performance, I am interested in how the dramatic crises arise out of, and develop through, several key moments, especially those which involve the Weird Sisters, the relationship between Macbeth and Lady Macbeth, and how these might become manifest in a production.

It is not clear where we are at the beginning of *Macbeth*. Typically, the First Folio of 1623, in which this Scottish play first appeared, leaves the question of scenic location open to actors', producers' and directors' interpretations. '*Thunder and lightning. Enter three witches*' are the only clues that are offered. It is not until scene three when Macbeth asks them 'why / Upon this blasted heath you stop our way / With such prophetic greeting?'[1] that the audience is given a sense of geographical location, and it is not forced to be the same as the opening scene. A heath it might well be, but it is also one of non-specific form. We learn that the witches vanish into air, 'as breath into the wind,' and that 'The earth hath bubbles as the water has, / And these are of them.' (1.3. 80 and 77-78). Earth, air, and water. Fire might strike at any moment with the lightning flash, if not brought up from Hell with the witches themselves: a quality that Hamlet perceives in the presence of his father's ghost, in Shakespeare's other tragedy about a King who is murdered.

No one, it seems, can approach *Macbeth*, except through the unholy trinity of these figures. A production will need to decide how far it wants to explore the degree of control that the witches are shown to have over dramatic events, and how far, if at all, they might appear in other ways and forms, perhaps when least expected, as the narrative unfolds. The opening might decide to attach greater prominence to the political landscape, so that when we hear of 'When the battle's lost and won', we already have a sense of that combat, and who is involved. *Macbeth* is presenting a world in which the supernatural governs the natural; in which all things visible and invisible compete for cosmic, as well as worldly power; and in which a King shows deep fascination in witchcraft: just as James I himself did.

The witches have to be every bit as frightening to grown-ups in Shakespeare's play as they are to the childish imagination. How they appear, how they speak, how they move are all crucial to the effect of fear they might achieve live in a theatre. Are they old, young, or do they encompass a range of ages that might then speak to a range of worldly experience? The witches are the only characters to use diverse kinds of poetic metre. We hear them speaking in iambic tetrameter as well as pentameter. How do they interact with each other and respond to these vocal challenges of their roles? Do they speak out to the audience and make us part of their world, casting a spell over our imaginary forces? Witches they might be in the stage directions, but Weird Sisters is their most common form of reference in the dialogue. 'Weird' comes from the Anglo-Saxon meaning 'Fate'. Their classical counterparts are the three Fates: Clotho (the Spinner), Lachesis (the Drawer of Lots), and Atropos (the Inevitable).

The theatrical and fantastic spirit of how the witches might make an impact on an audience is captured well by a former Poet Laureate, John Masefield. He published *A Macbeth Production* in 1945, intended as a handbook to amateur performances staged in the new period of peace, post-World War Two. Masefield's charming book advises actors about the characters' historical counterparts, suggests which tartan might be worn, and also gives advice about staging choices. On the witches, he assumes that the production will start with musical accompaniment, and writes:

> Let the music and the song be dread; and their appearance bring shudder. Be very careful to make the scene one of intense poetry, to show that these are unearthly beings in touch with terrible life, which cries and croaks to them out of the air. It is a little scene of forty seconds which you must make men remember forever. Friends, do not let your witches laugh; Satan's kingdom does not laugh.[2]

The relationship of the Weird Sisters to the many aspects of their play-world is crucial for a production to establish, and Shakespeare provides ample opportunity with the three of them starting off the theatrical events with a bang, and re-appearing to cast a spell for a tempest at sea, about seventy lines later in act one scene three. Not only do they represent the most important key with which an audience is invited to unlock the complexities of *Macbeth*, the Weird Sisters are also a rich site of theatrical meaning in the opportunities they afford for doubling with other characters. Since they apparently straddle both genders in appearance – 'You should be women; / And yet your beards forbid me to interpret / That you are so' (1.3.43-45) – their appearance also raises questions about how far a production might explore issues of gender in relation to tragedy. One of them could double with Lady Macbeth (who turns herself into a sort of witch after reading her husband's report of them), or she herself might double with Hecate, the Wicked Queen of the Witches (thus portraying an altogether deeper and even more sinister control of Macbeth on his wife's part). The portrayal of the Weird Sisters might become associated with other areas of a production through the use of lighting and sound. The role of the Devil-Porter could be easily double with one of them, and they might enter and exit through the same trap door. It would be possible to double Macduff and Lennox with the other two, so that all three would appear on stage, inside the Castle of Inverness to welcome Macbeth a few moments before the discovery of Duncan's body: 'Our knocking has awaked him: here he comes' (2.3.42). This would also mean that one of the Weird Sisters (Macduff) would also be responsible for the death of Macbeth. So, the abstract nature of the opening scene of *Macbeth* raises many questions and issues that a production will need to think through carefully, the answers to which will affect levels of meaning throughout in relation to the Weird Sisters, who after all, underpin not only the story, but the entire structure of the drama.

No sooner have the Weird Sisters cleared the stage – or *do* they clear the stage? – than we see a King enter with his retinue, and hear him speak about a man of blood. Blood is at the heart of the system of monarchy, and it is no coincidence that that institution should appear on stage in such close proximity to the Weird Sisters. King Duncan remarks upon a man covered in blood. He, too, will be covered in blood just seven scenes later. It is as if this Bloody Captain is a personal apparition and prophecy for King Duncan himself, perhaps made possible by the Weird Sisters' opening incantation. Perhaps the Weird Sisters are seen making, constructing, or conjuring up the Bloody Captain before leaving him on stage as a personal apparition for King Duncan. In the next scene we learn they are 'Posters of the sea and land,' (1.3. 31) and this might find literal expression through them being travellers around the very stage itself, weaving together political events, and determining encounters for the political protagonists.

What is King Duncan like? Old and graceful? Old and tyrannical? Much respected and the source of humour for his court? King Duncan's meekness and saintly qualities – 'His silver skin laced with his golden blood' (2.3.

112) – are the perceptions of Macbeth, products of his personal and public exaggerations. His point of view is prompted by him seeking to justify the murder of the grooms, and in seeking to avoid suspicion. The depiction of Duncan might strongly relate to the presentation of Scotland in a production. Do we see any kind of religious system being portrayed? How saintly *is* Duncan? This possible quality is thrown into relief in act four scene three with the English Doctor's report of the English King Edward I (the Confessor) curing those sick of an affliction known as the Evil, with the sanctified touch of his royal hands. Malcolm goes on to detail these miraculous cures to Macduff; this is one kingly quality he has not apparently inherited, nor is it known of in Scotland. How royal do we see King Duncan being? This is the role to which Macbeth aspires, but what might the audience find attractive about it? Rich robes, fanfares, and luxury, or an exhausted King on a battlefield, and head of a war-weary nation? Our first impressions of King Duncan are also connected to our first impressions of Macbeth as we hear of his achievements and butchery in war, making him, like Coriolanus, a reputed warrior and 'thing of blood,'[3] another bloody captain.

The way in which Macbeth first enters is crucial to the audience's understanding of his mental and emotional pre-disposition. Derek Jacobi, who played Macbeth in the 1993 RSC production, believes that:

> the speed with which things happen in the next phase of the play is to a large extent conditioned by Macbeth's physical and mental state when he receives the witches' greeting (. . .) He has been killing all day: he is covered with blood (. . .) I didn't want to show a man exhausted by battle, but revelling in it; a man in his glory, a great power house. 'So foul and fair a day' does not, it seems to me, refer to the weather: 'foul' is about those heads he's cut off and bowels he's ripped out; 'fair' is because it was all worth it, for this great glory.[4]

The text does not provide much room for manoeuvre or growth in the portrayal of its central character. In his immediate reactions to the greetings and prophecies of the Weird Sisters, the actor playing Macbeth needs to express a sudden and external change. Over just eight lines (lines 48-55) from Macbeth's surprise to hear that he'll become King, to Banquo's observation that 'he seems rapt withal,' (1.3. 53) we have one of the main challenges of the play in miniature. The space allowed for Macbeth's tragic journey is short, but the significance of each destination en route is immense, and somehow the actor has to convince the audience that he is arriving at each point in turn, *and to take us with him*. Does the actor listen to the prophecies made about Banquo, or does he use those eleven lines (lines 55-65) visibly to hurtle towards the soliloquy he speaks as an aside just thirty-eight lines later, after he is awarded the title Thane of Cawdor (line 103)? Towards the end of the scene the language of externalised emotion becomes part of Macbeth's and the audience's dramatic understanding of his journey:

> Why do I yield to that suggestion
> Whose horrid image doth unfix my hair
> And make my seated heart knock at my ribs
> Against the use of nature? Present fears
> Are less than horrible imaginings.
> My thought, whose murder yet is but fantastical,
> Shakes so my single state of man that function
> Is smothered in surmise, nothing is
> But what is not. (1.3. 133-41)

These are difficult words which might leave the audience pondering their meaning for some time after they have been spoken. Combining Macbeth's physical with his emotional reactions is an important part of the gauntlet that Shakespeare throws down to any actor willing to take it up. From a brave, bold, and greatly honoured warrior, to a man contemplating murder and a throne, Macbeth has now entered a frame of mind and way of being that totally negates any civilised, moral structures or codes of conduct, and all this over the course of just one hundred and two lines since his entrance (from line 36 to line 138).

Just before Macbeth's next entrance, Shakespeare gives an acting company one of his helpfully ironic stage directions. After enquiring about the death of the treacherous Thane of Cawdor, King Duncan admits that 'he was a gentleman on whom I built / An absolute trust.' (1.4.14). Immediately he's said this, Macbeth enters, interrupting Duncan's speech, and changing its direction on the half line. It is comparable to the entrance of '*Orlando bearing Adam*' in *As You Like It*, just after Jacques's famous speech about mankind's seven ages: 'Sans teeth, sans eyes, sans taste, sans everything.'[5] In both cases Shakespeare brings onto the stage characters who undercut by their very presence the tone of the speeches we have just heard. The conflict between Duncan's words and Macbeth's intentions continues through the scene. It is always worth watching out for Macbeth's reactions when Duncan proclaims Malcolm the Prince of Cumberland, and heir to his throne. Malcolm is not given anything to say, which a production might use to question his suitability for kingship. Macbeth must hide his reactions, or does he give anything away? Does anyone on stage notice a momentary slippage of Macbeth's mask of duty? Is it a moment of humour? How does Macbeth respond to Malcolm, and how is the news received by everyone else? Duncan continues the dramatic conflict by inviting Macbeth to host a royal visit at Inverness Castle. Macbeth exits on a powerful aside and two rhyming couplets, taking the audience's attention with him. Macbeth now self-consciously enters the realm of darkness, making there a space for himself alone:

> Stars, hide your fires,
> Let not light see my black and deep desires;
> The eye wink at the hand; yet let that be
> Which the eye fears, when it is done, to see. (1.4. 50-53)

The stars will indeed *not* be shining on the night of the killing. By contrast, King Duncan, whose speech concludes the scene, does not rhyme. He is left floundering with half lines, looking forward to the feast, over which the audience can superimpose his death:

> Let's after him,
> Whose care is gone before to bid us welcome.
> It is a peerless kinsman. (1.4. 56-58)

Our ears are still ringing with Macbeth's rhyming couplets, which automatically undercut and upstage Duncan's dramatic impact. Shakespeare has Macbeth overreaching himself in verbal structures, as well as in the narrative action.

We see Lady Macbeth first enter in the same way as we see her finally exit: caught up in her own world and private imaginings. She enters with a letter. Is she reading it? Can we tell whether she is reading it for the first time, or whether she is studying its contents after careful reflection? If the former, then we have a Lady Macbeth who is impetuous, and easily swayed by her own instincts; if the latter, then a production can impress more her premeditation of the crime. Importantly, she enters reading her husband's words, and the audience might catch their first glimpse of their marriage depending on Lady Macbeth's responses. In her following soliloquy, she speaks of chastising her husband with the 'valour of [her] tongue,' (1.5. 26) and depending on the casting, any power she has over Macbeth might begin to be apparent in her physical appearance, her age, her tone of voice. Her invocation of evil spirits can be a moment of fear as much for the character, as for the actress and the audience. 'She has spoke what she should not (. . .) Heaven knows what she has known.'(5.1. 46-47). These words of the waiting gentlewoman are just as pertinent here as they are in a much later scene, when she attends her sleepwalking mistress. Lady Macbeth seems to encounter some kind of unholy annunciation, as her entire being – the sense of her own sexuality, and womanhood – is caught up in her resolve to kill. Her desire to be enwrapped by night and hell will become painfully true for her during her later nightmares when she sees that 'Hell is murky.' (5.1. 34).

On Macbeth's entrance, Shakespeare allows us to see husband and wife together for the first time. Just how far we are allowed insights into the Macbeths' marriage in a production might have a proportional effect on how much sympathy we feel for them. Has Lady Macbeth goaded her husband in quite this same way before? Lady Macbeth speaks sixteen and a half out of an all too brief eighteen and a half lines of dialogue. She is taking control, but how does Macbeth respond to her advice? Is he afraid of her? Do we perceive any stage echoes of the way we saw him contemplate the Weird Sisters? Or, perhaps he is quietly confident and satisfied that his wife is reflecting back to him what we have already seen him realise for himself.

The next few scenes require a flexible playing space. Duncan arrives at the Castle and notices its pleasant prospect and climate. It seems important to Shakespeare to make this contrast; there has already been much metaphorical darkness up to this point. With the sun shining, Lady Macbeth can seem even more like the 'innocent flower' as she enters to greet King Duncan. The scene then apparently changes to evening and Macbeth's next soliloquy is spoken while the King is at supper. The literal, scenic location becomes darker as we move closer towards the murder. Importantly this speech contains a vision of angels and of the heavens opening:

> Besides, this Duncan
> Hath borne his faculties so meek, hath been
> So clear in his great office, that his virtues
> Will plead like angels, trumpet-tongued against
> The deep damnation of his taking-off,
> And pity, like a naked new-born babe,
> Striding the blast, or heaven's cherubin, horsed
> Upon the sightless couriers of the air,
> Shall blow the horrid deed in every eye
> That tears shall drown the wind. (1.7. 16-25)

If we are to see Macbeth falling from the heavens, Lucifer-like, then now is the time for a production to show that. Here is a man capable of experiencing a deity, possibly with the help of the angels themselves, and who is then able to turn away, Faustus-like, and move towards everlasting damnation instead. Lady Macbeth interrupts his musings with her final persuasions. Notice how it is her speech which doubts Macbeth's manhood and recalls her suckling infant child which moves her husband forward from 'Who dares do more is none' to 'If we should fail?' Somewhere during that speech, his resolve is strengthened. Did the child Lady Macbeth refers to die? Is this one aspect of the on-going, unspoken pain of experience which constitutes their marriage, and is it through this that Macbeth finds resolve?

The use of the upper-stage space in the Globe Theatre might have provided a vantage point for Banquo's watch at the beginning of act two, with Macbeth speaking up to him from the lower stage. During his soliloquy about the imagined dagger the entire playing space and auditorium become an extension of Macbeth's own state of mind and provide scope for his horrible imaginings. We see a man tortured by self-isolation, for whom the invisible, supernatural world, once again, becomes momentarily visible.

The urgent and dangerous dialogue that the Macbeths share just after the murder of King Duncan needs only to be delivered with the constant threat of discovery for it to be electrifying. It is a crucial point in Macbeth's development. The audience might begin to perceive glimmers of not only how dangerous he could become, but also how Lady Macbeth might no longer be able to exert her influence over him. In fact, this is the last time we see them together on stage when Lady Macbeth *does* command control over him. What changes the balance is not only Macbeth's increasing paranoia, but also the plain fact that she returns to take the daggers back to the scene of the crime and smear the grooms' faces with Duncan's blood. What she sees will haunt her sleeping moments, and fathom the depths of her humanity. As we see Lady Macbeth finding her voice of humanity and pity in her tormented dreams, we see Macbeth losing his, and becoming less and less sensitive to the horrors for which he is responsible.

And then there is knocking on the door, and an absurdly comic interlude with the Porter. Audiences look forward to the Porter scene. In the theatre you can almost hear the audience settling down to enjoy it at soon as he appears. Linguistically, his lines about how drink 'provokes the desire but it takes away the performance [...it] makes him stand to and not stand to' (2.3. 27-28 and 33) can draw knowing laughter whether or not they are accompanied by bawdy gestures signifying male tumescence and detumescence, no doubt appropriate when there is so much 'knocking' around the stage (in the obvious sexual sense of the word). On a linguistic level, most of the Porter's speech is relatively obscure, and the actor might be encouraged simply to be as amusing as possible, even to ad-lib, ingratiating himself like a stand-up comedian with the audience. In 1987, Declan

Donnellan's Cheek By Jowl production included a drunk and swearing female Porter, who made jokes about stockbrokers and the Minister for Health. Stephen Noonan's Porter in Gregory Doran's 1999 RSC production provides an interesting example of an improvised Porter in what was clearly understood to be in the spirit of Shakespeare's original. Taking as his point of departure that the Porter is really concerned with 'some of all professions that go the primrose way to the everlasting bonfire,' (2.3. 17-18). Noonan surprised audience members in the Swan Theatre by staring at them whilst sounding disconcertingly modern: 'What are you?' He no doubt expected replies such as 'a teacher', 'a nurse', 'a student'. One night when asked 'What are you?' a red-faced man replied 'embarrassed'. It brought the house down. Noonan's equivocator also led him into a not unconvincing impersonation of Tony Blair: 'I am totally and one hundred per cent committed to the idea of equivocation.' Also, the Porter is often the only character in a production to speak with a Scottish accent. Offensive this certainly is, if you are from north of the border, as it assumes that there is something intrinsically amusing about a Scottish accent, which is hilarious when spoken by a drunken Scot.

And yet, to adapt the Porter scene in these ways is to mis-remember it and to ignore the script as printed. Improvised versions of the scene assume that Shakespeare's original clown actor would have probably ad-libbed his way through the scene anyway, and that the scene as we have it represents only one version of the event which happened to be recorded, or the scene before the clown actor got to it. Far from being an episode which can easily be substituted by improvisation and knockabout or stand-up comedy, the Porter scene can be taken seriously and reflected back onto the rest of the play. This is not to ignore that the scene is comic, but to acknowledge that its comedy, as scripted, is differently sophisticated to the way that many productions understand it to be. There is every reason to play the Porter with utmost seriousness; his bawdy jokes will take care of themselves. After all, he talks about Hell and invents the verb 'to devil porter' (a compound form still absent from the *Oxford English Dictionary*). There is every reason to suppose that he is a further representation of the supernatural on stage, a metaphor for the Devil himself, opening the gate of Hell irrevocably on to the play, and wider on to the mind and emotions of the Macbeths.

A coronation has taken place sometime between the end of act two scene three and act three scene one. Does the production lavish this event on the Macbeths, and do we see them enjoying their magisterial privileges for a short while? It does not seem long before Macbeth realises that killing brings on more killing, and that he'll need to wade further into the blood of others, if he is to maintain his own position of power. Lady Macbeth, too, is granted her own small moment of soliloquy, during which an audience can catch a glimpse of her developing state of mind. Cut off from her husband, she has to ask her servant for the news about Banquo's absence from court. And then she delivers just two rhyming couplets while she is alone on stage:

> Naught's had, all's spent,
> Where our desire is got without content.
> 'Tis safer to be that which we destroy
> Than by destruction dwell in doubtful joy. (3.2. 6-9)

It is possible to see the seeds of what will later become, by Macbeth, a fully articulated nihilism; it also possible to perceive Lady Macbeth's mind already contemplating suicide: she has gained nothing, there is nothing else to strive for, and she has lost all her chances. From the dialogue that follows with Macbeth, it seems that she is going on for the sake of her husband, who neither needs nor wants the support she can offer. One of the most difficult lines for an actor playing Macbeth is the sudden, terrifying, and heart-wrenching insight that suddenly flashes out of nowhere when he confesses: 'O, full of scorpions is my mind, dear wife!' (3.2. 37). It is a moment of searing submission for the character, even more so because the detail seems hopelessly isolated from its immediate context. For an actor, the line might open a gash of vulnerability in his performance which can sting and solicit the audience's immediate sympathy, but only if he can make them believe it, otherwise we have a Macbeth who is continuing on his tragic course alone. For Lady Macbeth, the phrase probably instils an even greater insecurity than she felt at the beginning of the scene, and now she is the one left asking the question: 'What's to be done?' (3.2. 45) which Macbeth refuses to answer. She can only marvel at her husband's words.

The banquet at which the ghost of Banquo appears – is he literally embodied, or do we see the actor playing Macbeth imagining he's seen a ghost? – really marks the end of the Macbeths' relationship, at least in stage terms. The audience will not see them together again after this point. Shakespeare leaves open the possibility that Lady Macbeth herself might also see the Ghost of Banquo. If this were to be the case, then the audience would see the return of her initial steely resolve, as she looks upon the Ghost, but manages to maintain her countenance. Sian Thomas played Lady Macbeth and Gertrude in the 2004 RSC season: the only other female role in the Shakespeare canon who is present on stage when a ghost appears, and who might or might not see it.

The dialogue between King and Queen, husband and wife, after the banquet brilliantly suggests Lady Macbeth's blank resignation and exhaustion. The time of day is utterly unimportant to her, and the night is 'Almost at odds with morning, which is which.' (3.4. 126). Her non-specific, perhaps even nonchalant remark, somehow also manages to convey that she has enough self-knowledge to realise that the best of life is over for her. Shakespeare also dramatises here two people who fluctuate between reacting to each other, and speaking to themselves from an intensely private, disconnected perspective. Macbeth has a vision of blood, and pauses to ask his wife the time. She replies and he asks her, instead, what it was that she said about Macduff not attending the feast. Her line, 'You lack the season of all natures, sleep' (3.4. 140) is the first compassionate statement she has made thus far in the play. It is like Lear's 'How dost, my boy? Art cold?'[6] when he shows pity to someone else (the Fool) other than himself. Macbeth's concluding '*We* are yet but young in deed,' might encompass the first person plural, and might suggest an attempt to re-connect with his wife on his part, but it seems to be too little, too late. Do they leave the stage together? Do we see a mutually supportive, though world-weary, man and woman take hold of each other with pity, or does Macbeth still want to keep himself isolated? In the 1999 RSC production, Lady Macbeth (Harriet Walter) took up a candle from the banquet table, life's brief candle, that she would always want beside her in the night during her tormented sleep.

And that's where we arrive at now. Passing over the apparitions and Macbeth's further, darker communion with the Weird Sisters, the political crises facing Scotland and England, the slaughter of Macduff's family, and the grief of Macduff himself (who, lest we forget, suffers the greatest, personal, loss in this tragedy) we come to Lady Macbeth's sleepwalking scene. The ordinary and loyal duty of the Doctor and Gentlewoman provide a directness and openness of dialogue in prose, comparable to that between Lady Macduff and her son. Framing an extraordinary scene of ultimate breakdown and penetrating insight, the two observers create a bridge from Lady Macbeth's nightmare to the audience. A production will be able to determine just how far an audience can make connections between what Lady Macbeth sees and hears in her sleep, and what the audience saw earlier on stage. Her observation that 'Hell is murky' is both comic in its degree of understatement, and utterly terrifying in it being a voice of humanity struggling against its own personal torment. But it is her observation '*Yet-who-would-have-thought-the-old-man-to-have-had-so-much-blood-in-him*?' that is perhaps the most disarming (5.1. 36-38). Her eyewitness account patters out in monosyllables, which the actor can speak as slowly or as quickly as the moment warrants. Here Lady Macbeth refers to an imagined, off-stage reality that only she was privy to when she returned with the daggers and smeared Duncan's blood over the sleeping grooms. The sigh, signified only by the exclamatory 'O, O, O,' in the text, can be as terrible or as pathetic as the actor chooses. The sinister Porter appears again as an implied presence in her nightmares as the knocking on the south entry echoes through the castle from two acts earlier, like an irregular heart-beat, or the blood pulsating in her ears with fear:

> To bed, to bed. There's a knocking at the gate. Come, come, come, come, give me your hand. What's done cannot be undone. To bed, to bed, to bed.
> (5.1. 63-65)

Or as Harriet Walter would have it: 'I wanted the audience to feel they were eavesdropping on Lady Macbeth cocooned in her private Hell.'[7] Here we see Lady Macbeth terrified of the dark, like a child, always wanting light by her. Her journey from her having scorned Macbeth because he was afraid to return to Duncan's body – 'The sleeping and the dead / Are but as pictures. 'Tis the eye of childhood / That fears a painted devil' – is now at an end. (2.2. 51-53). We even hear a pathetic moment of tragic childish nursery rhyme: 'The Thane of Fife had a wife, where is she now?' (5.1. 40-41). To paraphrase the famous essay by the great Sir Francis Bacon, Lady Macbeth fears death (both her own and other people's) as children fear the dark. Death, even the very smell of it, has become the same as the dark to her, and both are equally terrifying.

Macbeth requires a dramatic momentum of fear. Caught up in this 'supernatural soliciting' are Shakespeare's original underpinning framework of the Weird Sisters, the political well-being of a nation state, the marriage of the Macbeths, and their interconnected, but in the end distinct tragic journeys. The old Lord Lafeu in *All's Well That Ends Well* opens act two scene three with some lines which it is tempting to think represent Shakespeare's own world view. Whether or not they do will never be known, but they are, I think, worth pencilling in the margins of how we approach *Macbeth* as both a text and as a performance.

> They say miracles are past, and we have our philosophical persons to make modern and familiar things supernatural and causeless. Hence it is that we make trifles of terrors, ensconcing ourselves into seeming knowledge when we should submit ourselves to an unknown fear.[8]

Antony Sher, who played Macbeth in the 1999 RSC production, recalls how members of the company

> were asked to describe their own experiences of ultimate fear. An astonishing range of stories emerged: natural disasters, near-fatal accidents, deep-seated phobias, recurring dreams. These sessions were often gruelling and upsetting to sit through. But if we were to do justice to the heart of this play, if we were to contact the *reality* of terror, we would have to open ourselves to some unpalatable stuff.[9]

The challenges implicit in Shakespeare's shortest tragedy have been requiring actors and audiences to submit to the fear it instills for four hundred years. And it is up to each new production of *Macbeth* to help us sup full of horrors afresh, and taste its fears, as the terrible tale unfolds.

Notes

[1] William Shakespeare, *The Complete Works*, ed. by Stanley Wells, Gary Taylor, John Jowett and William Montgomery (Oxford: Clarendon Press, 1988; repr. 1995), *Macbeth*, 1.3.74-76. All quotations from Shakespeare are taken from this edition.
[2] John Masefield, *A Macbeth Production* (London: William Heinemann, 1945), p. 34.
[3] *Coriolanus*, 2.2.109
[4] Derek Jacobi, 'Macbeth', in Robert Smallwood (ed.), *The Players of Shakespeare 4* (Cambridge: Cambridge University Press, 1998), pp. 193-210 (pp. 197 and 195).
[5] *As You Like It*, 2.7.166
[6] *The Tragedy of King Lear*, 3.2.68
[7] Harriet Walter, *Macbeth*, Actors on Shakespeare series (London: Faber and Faber), p. 57.
[8] *All's Well That Ends Well*, 2.3.1-6
[9] Antony Sher, 'Leontes in *The Winter's Tale*, and Macbeth', in Robert Smallwood (ed.), *Players of Shakespeare 5* (Cambridge: Cambridge University Press, 2003), pp. 91-112 (p.104).

AS THEY LIKED IT:

DEPARTURES FROM SHAKESPEARE'S TEXT IN TWO ADAPTATIONS OF *AS YOU LIKE IT*

Viggo Hjørnager Pedersen

As Paul V. Rubow observes, the bookshelves are groaning with works on Shakespeare's influence abroad,[1] and there are certainly a number of studies of Shakespeare in Denmark.[2] Likewise, there is no end of studies of Shakespeare's romantic comedies. However, studies that combine a reinterpretation of the original with translation studies are perhaps not quite so numerous, and that is the reason why I have dared to embark on a limited, but – to me at least – interesting investigation of some of the reasons that consciously or unconsciously motivated the Danish translator and dramatist Sille Beyer (1803-61) to rewrite *As You Like It* as *Livet i Skoven* [*Life in the Forest*].[3] This study also makes passing reference to George Sand's *Comme il vous plaira*[4] (1858) which is strangely parallel to the Danish adaptation.

Sille Beyer's work is discussed in the context of stage history by Birgit Gad.[5] She argues convincingly that in order to please an audience fed on Eugène Scribe, Shakespeare had to be 'systematised' and made lighter, and that characters were altered or discarded to fit in with the demands of a tighter plot and the limitations imposed by the actors available at the Royal Theatre in Copenhagen. When, for instance, Celia was made more prominent and interesting in the Danish version than in the original, this was because the part was wanted by Johanne Louise Heiberg, the leading lady of the theatre and wife of the director. Gad even quotes Heiberg for a critique of *The Merchant of Venice* where he justifies rewriting the classics to fit in with the taste of the present,[6] and Sille Beyer quotes Heiberg as the authority who emboldened her to undertake a rewriting of *Twelfth Night*.[7]

Undoubtedly this is very true. But when one looks at the play as a literary text rather than simply as the basis for a theatrical production, what strikes one is that the end result of the changes is to remove the counter-pattern to the idyllic love stories that take place as it were on the surface of *As You Like It* – a pattern that has struck me more and more as I have discussed the play with students over the years, but which is not generally acknowledged, at least in the notes and commentaries found in the Arden edition and similar sources.

Sille Beyer

Sille Beyer was the daughter of an academic turned merchant. She was mostly privately educated, if not self-taught, and she used her ten years as lady companion to a widow to devote more time to her studies and to literature than most women of that epoch. Her first play was performed at the Royal Theatre in 1832, at about the time when she began to translate for the theatre. She knew French, Spanish, Italian and some English – just how much is difficult to say. German, on the other hand, goes without saying – indeed, at that period educated Danes read a fair amount of foreign literature in German, Shakespeare included.

Sille Beyer's adaptation of *As You Like It* may seem a little less radical than her *Viola* (i.e. *Twelfth Night*), where, much to the disgust of Rubow, among others,[8] she edits out the entire Malvolio plot. Still, her adaptation departs from Shakespeare so far that it is difficult to say how much she used his own text, if at all. Most of the adaptation could easily be derived from Schlegel's German version,[9] which unlike Sille Beyer's Danish version, follows Shakespeare reasonably closely. There were also earlier Danish translations, notably that of Wulff.[10] Still, as we shall see, there are passages in Beyer which are closer to Shakespeare (see below), and Gad demonstrates that on one occasion at least Beyer commented on a discrepancy between a German translation and Shakespeare's English, which leads her to believe that Beyer did indeed translate from English.[11] A short summary of Beyer's plot (for it is not Shakespeare's) might help to prepare the ground for a discussion of her version.

Livet i Skoven

I   From the wrestling match to the departure of Celia and Rosalind. Oliver has already been banished, so his cruelty to his brother is erased. The whole sequence is slightly shortened.

II   From the introduction of Duke Senior in the forest to the reception of Adam and Orlando. The songs have been cut, as has Jacques, and Touchstone's role is much reduced.

III   From the scene at the castle following the girls' departure to a conversation between them (largely added by Sille Beyer). Orlando's poems on the trees are there, but the parody is by Celia, not Touchstone, and is fairly demure. We see the brothers in amiable conversation. Oliver, who has taken over the function of the missing Jacques, is falling in love with Celia.

IV   From Rosalind upbraiding Orlando for being late to the conclusion of the play, where no Hymen appears. This act is disproportionately long. The reigning duke has gone to the forest and is denounced by his followers, who change allegiance. He is attacked by a boar, but saved by Orlando. In the end there are only three couples – Touchstone remains single, as Audrey has been edited out together with William. The play ends with the reconciliation of the two dukes, as the banished duke forgives his brother.

To sum up, the misanthropy of Jacques, the scurrility of Touchstone and the witty but worldly if not cynical repartee of the girls are all omitted, as are the songs with their suggestive atmosphere. On the other hand, as we shall see, sometimes Beyer is quite close to Shakespeare's text.

Shakespeare's Other Pattern
The usual understanding of *As You Like It* is that it is a witty comedy about the nature and conditions of love. It contains no fewer than four matches: two of love at first sight (Rosalind and Orlando, and Oliver and Celia: even though the love of the former couple develops into *amour d'estime*), one of service rewarded (Silvius and Phoebe), and one of convenience and sensuality (Touchstone and Audrey). Although this last couple illustrates the fact that not all 'love' is ideal, romantic love certainly preponderates, and is rewarded in the end by Hymen *ex machina*.

However, apart from Touchstone's cynicism, which masks his devotion to Celia (*amour courtois* without hope of reward), there is one utterly discordant voice, that of Jacques. And there is likewise a discordant note in the buffoonery, which goes ill with the idea of romantic love and might well tempt the classically minded to edit it out.

A gross example is Touchstone's 'from hour to hour we rot, and rot',[12] whose pun on 'hour' and 'whore' is one of many thinly veiled references to the effects of syphilis, which according to Fabricius[13] was a problem only too well known to Shakespeare, the most blatant example is probably Touchstone's parody of Orlando's eulogy on Rosalind:[14]

> If a hart do lack a hind,
> Let him seek out Rosalind.
> If the cat will after kind,
> So be sure will Rosalind.
> Winter's garments must be lin'd,
> So must slender Rosalind.
> They that reap must sheaf and bind,
> Then to cart with Rosalind.

Sweetest nut hath sourest rind,
Such a nut is Rosalind.
He that sweetest rose will find,
Must find love's prick, and Rosalind.

Sille Beyer enjoys the rhymes, but not the content, which she changes completely, assigning the speech to Celia:

Var der nu ikke flere Riim at finde?
Mig tykkes dog, at Rimet staaer paa Pinde,
Saasnart det gielder Navnet Rosalinde;
Og alle Digtets Toner maa sig spinde
I lette bløde Riim paa Rosalinde,
Der springe hurtigt frem som trinde Hinde,
Blandt alle Skovens Ege, Bøge, Linde –

On the other hand, here as elsewhere Schlegel translates fairly accurately:

Sehnt der Hirsch sich nach den Hinden
Lasst ihn suchen Rosalinden.
Will die Katze sich verbinden:
Glaubt, sie macht's gleich Rosalinden.
Reben müssen Bäum' umwinden:
So tut's nötig Rosalinden.
Wer da mäht, muss Garben binden:
Auf den Karr'n mit Rosalinden.
Süsse Nuss hat saure Rinden
Solche Nuss gleicht Rosalinden.
Wer süsse Rosen sucht, muss finden
Der Liebe Dorn, und Rosalinden.

Even if "der Liebe Dorn" is less obvious than "Love's prick", this is quite an astonishingly bitter diatribe against a nice young lady, the cousin and bosom-friend of Touchstone's mistress, Celia. Of course it is fun, and of course he is not railing against Rosalind but against the idea of romantic love, but even so. It certainly gives a new perspective to the idea of curing lovers of their passion, which is repeatedly associated with disease, and not always in fun, and it demonstrates that Jacques' more serious railings against love do not stand alone.

His reason for despising love is made public by Duke Senior:[15]

> For thou thyself hast been a libertine,
> As sensual as the brutish sting itself,
> And all the embossed sores and headed evils
> That thou with licence of free foot hast caught
> Wouldst thou disgorge into the general world.

Love also carries with it the fear or reality of faithlessness. In this play, Rosalind is not too sure of her Orlando's constancy, and Audrey certainly has no reason to trust Touchstone. But worse than that, a young man by the name of William – like the author of the play – is humiliated and driven away by Touchstone when he comes to pay his respects to Audrey.

This may well be an additional reason for the distrust of love in this play: the Audrey/William/Touchstone triangle unmistakably resembles the conflict in the sonnets; and I cannot recall any other instance of an author giving the simpleton of his text his own name. It looks very much like self-parody: William, a country bumpkin or upstart crow, is ousted by a self-important but shallow courtier while trying to retain the love of a worthless female. Not a very edifying spectacle in a love comedy; and of course the message does not survive in the two 19th-century translations discussed here, even if George Sand retains William; but then she has a use for him: he, not Touchstone, marries Audrey in the end.

In his private relations too, Touchstone certainly does his best to undermine the idea of romantic love: there is nothing romantic about his interest in Audrey, it is a case of 'cat will after kind'.

The various attitudes to love are summed up nicely by Hymen,[16] as he unites the four couples and at the same time comments on them:

> You and you no cross shall part,
> You and you are heart in heart,
> You to his love must accord,
> Or have a woman to your lord.
> You and you are sure together,
> As the winter to foul weather.

To us, these contrasts add richness to the picture Shakespeare draws of love, its manifestations and its consequences. To minds schooled in the French tradition, however, this was simply too messy, and to the 19th century stage it was anathema. The negative subtext is cut by both Beyer and George Sand, and my contention is that for the same reason the resulting play is diminished, whether or not the translators understood what they were doing.

It can be argued that the cuts are simply a result of editing the play in the interests of a more 'dramatic' presentation and a closer adherence to the classical form of comedy. However, I do think that George Sand's uneasiness about Shakespeare's "effrayant cynisme" described below indicates an awareness of tensions in the play that classically schooled dramatists and critics did not want in a comedy. "Tragical mirth" did not appeal to them.

The Criticism and Translation of George Sand

It is a curious fact, noted by Gad,[17] that in 1856 the French writer George Sand (1804-76) brought out a translation on similar lines as Beyer's, except that it is 'en trois actes et en prose'. Sille Beyer herself commented on this work, praising the preface which she thought contained ideas and feelings similar to her own of 10 years earlier.[18] Gad believes that the similarities must be coincidental, but I do not find it impossible that George Sand might in fact have heard of the Copenhagen production. Certainly she wishes

> que, sur d'autres scènes, d'autres artistes, d'autres croyants nous secondent, comme quelques-uns nous ont déja encouragés par leur example ....[19]

Be that as it may, the detailed deliberations of the French translator in her preface are interesting as a comment on a situation which must have been very similar in Paris and Copenhagen.

Again and again George Sand regrets having to treat the text in the way she does; she is well aware that much of Shakespeare's meaning is lost; referring to the 'poetical robe' of Shakespeare, she regrets "de ne pouvoir montrer cette robe toute entière aux yeux de notre public français moderne", and continues

> tout ceux qui ... connaissent Shakespeare savent bien que si elle est partout richement brodée, elle est parfois jeté sur l'épaule du dieu avec une negligence ou une audace qui ne sont plus de notre temps, et que notre goût ne supporterait pas.[20]

In her view, there are two reasons why it is necessary to revise Shakespeare: first, because his frankness in sexual matters simply cannot be imitated on a modern stage:

> Par un contraste étrange et qui semble incompréhensible, il a mis la grâce et la chasteté les plus divines à côté d'un plus effrayant cynisme, la douceur des anges auprès des fureurs du tigre, et la plus pénétrante douleur en face des intraduisibles *concetti* d'une audacieuse licence.

> Il n'y a donc pas moyen de traduire littéralement Shakespeare pour le théâtre, et si jamais il a été permis de résumer, d'extraire et d'expurger, c'est à l'égard de ce génie sauvage qui ne connait pas de frein.[21]

The second reason is that she finds Shakespeare's composition – not to put too fine a word upon it – sloppy; if Shakespeare is not readily appreciated in France,

> [c]'est la faute d'un progrès réel qui s'est fait dans l'art dramatique, et qui consiste principalement dans l'habileté du plan; il est certain que le moindre vaudeville de nos jours est mieux fait, sous ce rapport, que le plus admirable drames des maîtres du temps passé.[22]

Her own solution, which is similar to but by no means identical with that of Sille Beyer, is to expand the role of Celia and let her attract Jacques, who in the end is reformed and becomes a delighted bridegroom. At the same time, several minor characters are reduced or removed, and the 'intraduisibles *concetti*' are dropped.

Sille Beyer's Text
I think that on the whole Sille Beyer is a good dramatist, only she takes the liberty to use Shakespeare in the same way as he himself used his sources: with absolute freedom. Her text does not purport to be a translation: the title page proclaims it to be "En Bearbejdelse af Shakespeare's *As You Like It*", i.e. an adaptation of Shakespeare's play. For reasons similar to those of George Sand, with the critical approval of Heiberg, and influenced by the wishes of Mrs. Heiberg, Beyer gets rid of Jacques altogether, reduces the role of Touchstone, taking particular care to remove all sexual innuendo, and ekes out Celia's role with borrowed pieces of Rosalind's, and so forth. In so doing, she often paraphrases what she keeps, occasionally adding lines of her own. She writes a not unpleasing blank verse (even if her enjambments are perhaps not always well motivated), and she sometimes uses verse in places where Shakespeare does not.

The translation below of an excerpt from *As You Like It*,[23] where Rosalind first proposes to cure Orlando of his lovesickness, will serve to illustrate Beyer's technique. It will be noted that even though the translation is fairly free, the main ideas of the original are reproduced. But the tone is different – it is lyrical, where Shakespeare is witty and cynical, an effect which may partly be attributed to the substitution of blank verse for prose.

Rosalind
> There is a man haunts the forest that abuses our young plants with carving 'Rosalind' on their barks; hang odes upon hawthorns and elegies on brambles; all, forsooth, deifying the name of Rosalind. If I could meet that fancymonger, I would give him some good counsel, for he seems to have the quotidian of love upon him.

Rosalinde
> ... alle Træer her er mine Venner.
> Men kan I ikke sige mig, hvem kan
> Det være, der fordærver deres Bark,
> Og skærer Navnet Rosalinde ud
> I alle Stammer; og som hænger Vers
> Med Elskovsklager op paa hver en Quist?
> Hvis jeg ham traf, da tog jeg ham alvorligt
> I Kur, for denne Elskovsfeber.[24]

Occasionally, she comes even closer to the original, as in the discussion of the relativity of time,[25] where Rosalind's lines have been given to Celia. But even here there are characteristic changes:

Rosalind
> ... Time travels in divers paces with diverse persons. I'll tell you who Time ambles withal, who Time trots withal, who Time gallops withal, and who he stands still withal.

Celia
> Tiden gaaer forskjelligt med forskjellige Personer. Jeg kan sige Jer, hvem den gaaer i Fodgang med, og hvem den traver med, og hvem den løber i Gallop med, og hvem den staaer stille med.

Orlando
> I prithee, who doth he trot withal?

Orlando
> Siig mig da, hvem den traver med?

Rosalind
> Marry he trots hard with a young maid, between the contract of her marriage and the day it is solemnized. If the interim be but a se'nnight, Time's pace is so hard that it seems the length of seven years.

Celia
> Med en ung Pige, naar hun venter paa sin Elsker; om det kun er et Par Dage, saa synes hun dog det er hele Aar.

Orlando
> Who ambles Time withal?

Orlando
> Og hvem gaaer den i Fodgang med?

Rosalind
> With a priest that lacks Latin and a rich man that has not the gout, for the one sleeps easily because he cannot study, and the other lives merrily because he feels no pain, the one lacking the burden of lean and wasteful learning; the other knowing no burden of heavy tedious penury. These Time ambles withal.

Celia
> Med en Præst, som ikke kan Latin, og en riig Mand, som ingen Gigt har. Den Første, han tager sig det mageligt, fordi han kan ikke studere; og den Anden, han lever lystigt, fordi han ikke føler noget Ondt; og for hvem der ikke arbeider, gaaer Tiden altid i Fodgang.

Orlando
> Who doth he gallop withal?

Orlando
> Og hvem galloperer den med?

Rosalind
> With a thief to the gallows; for though he goes as softly as foot can fall, he thinks himself too soon there.

Celia
> Med en Tyv, naar han bliver ført til Galgen; vel gaaer han selv Fod for Fod, men han synes dog altid, at han kommer for tidligt.

Orlando
> Who stays he still withal?

Orlando
> Og hvem staaer den stille med?

Rosalind
> With lawyers in the vacation; for they sleep between term and term, and then they perceive not how time moves.

Celia
> Med en Øvrighedsperson, thi han sover i og udenfor Retten, og saa mærker han slet ikke at Tiden gaaer.

The substitution of "Øvrighedsperson" (public servant) for "lawyers" may well be due to Beyer's not understanding or not being able to find a translation for the idea of lawyers "sleeping from term to term". The remarks about ambling time show a tendency to shorten Shakespeare's text and get rid of some of the rhetoric, substituting a moral sentence with a nice *Biedermeyer* ring to it. But it is clearly a wish to avoid references to sexuality which leads the Danish text to substitute a girl waiting for the appearance of her lover for a bride longing for her wedding night.

Altogether, the changes introduced by George Sand and Sille Beyer, and the motivations given for them, tend to confirm Romy Heylen's findings that translators tend to adapt their texts to the literary norms of their culture.[26] The translations studied here are clearly influenced by the thinking of the age in which they were produced.

Conclusion

Sille Beyer's adaptations belong to a time when Shakespeare was still being (re)discovered, and when the knowledge of English abroad was generally very limited. With the translations of Edward Lembcke,[27] the Danish stage returned to using translations rather than adaptations of Shakespeare, even if Lembcke also tended to tone down sexual innuendo. But Sille Beyer's work was not lost. It was successful on the stage in its time, helped to pave the way for acceptance of the "real" Shakespeare, and in fact many of its formulations influenced or even survived in Lembcke's text; after all, the play *is* called *As You Like It*, and most audiences like a romantic play with a happy ending and not too many dissatisfied characters sulking on the sidelines.

Notes

[1] Paul V. Rubow, *Shakespeare på dansk* (Copenhagen: Levin og Munksgaard, 1932), p. 9.

[2] Rubow, *op.cit.*, has a thorough discussion of Shakespeare in Denmark up to his own time. After that, there have been several retranslations for individual performances, a translation of part of the canon by Johannes Sløk (1972-86), and a revised version of Lembcke's Shakespeare by Anne Chaplin Hansen *et al.* (*Samlede Shakespeare: Dramatiske Værker*. Copenhagen: Haase, 1978-84). The most notable development of recent times has been the new translations by Niels Brunse, still incomplete, which, hopefully, will eventually constitute a new Danish standard text.

[3] Sille Beyer, *Livet i Skoven: Romantisk Lystspil i 4 Acter* (Copenhagen: J.H. Schubothe's Boghandling, 1849).

[4] George Sand, *Comme il vous plaira* (Paris: Librairie Nouvelle, 1858).

[5] Birgit Gad, *Sille Beyers bearbejdelse af William Shakespeares lystspil* (Copenhagen: Gad, 1974).

[6] See Gad, pp. 13-14.

[7] Sille Beyer, *Viola* (Copenhagen: J.H. Schubothe's Boghandling, 1850), Introduction, p. III.

8   Rubow, pp. 30-31. Summing up, he rather unkindly says of Beyer: 'Med sine små hårde guvernante-hænder tog hun sig af hans [i.e. Shakespeare's] opdragelse, så han kom artig og striglet indtil det ukendelige ud af instituttet.'
9   A. Schlegel, *Wie es euch gefällt* (1799)(Stuttgart: Reclam (no year)).
10 P.F. Wulff, *William Shakespeares tragiske Værker* (Copenhagen: 1819).
11 Gad, p. 37.
12 William Shakespeare, *As You Like It*, ed. by Agnes Latham (1975), Arden Edition (London: Routledge, 1989 ff.), II.IV.27.
13 J. Fabricius, *Shakespeare's Hidden World* (Copenhagen: Munksgaard, 1989) and *Syphilus - den dystre fårehyrde* (Copenhagen: Den almindelige danske lægeforening, 1989), Bibliotek for læger, Medicinsk forum, 42. årgang, hæfte 4.
14 Shakespeare, III.II.99 ff.
15 *Ibid.* II.VII.65 ff.
16 *Ibid.* V.IV.125 ff.
17 Gad, pp. 37-46.
18 *Ibid.* p. 39.
19 Sand, p. 18.
20 *Ibid.* p.6.
21 *Ibid.* p. 13.
22 *Ibid.* p. 7.
23 Shakespeare, III.II.303-27.
24 Beyer, *Livet i Skoven*, p. 55.
25 Shakespeare, III.II.302-27.
26 Romy Heylen, *Translation, Poetics, & the Stage. Six French Hamlets* (London and New York: Routledge, 1993).
27 Edward Lembcke, *Shakespeares Samlede Dramatiske Værker* (Copenhagen: Gyldendal, 1910-11).

THE SPIRIT OF TRANSFORMATION:

SHAKESPEARE'S *THE TEMPEST* AND KAREN BLIXEN'S 'TEMPESTS'

Niels Bugge Hansen

The 'Afterlife' of *The Tempest* is uncommonly rich and varied, even for a Shakespearean text, as V. M. and A. T. Vaughan, the editors of the play in the new Arden Shakespeare series,[1] explain; however their careful and thorough account of a wide variety of literary and dramatic offshoots and critical, philosophical and sociological appropriations by no means exhausts the multitude of texts stemming in one way or another from Shakespeare's fertile drama. *The Tempest* is a key text for the study of appropriations of Shakespeare. Karen Blixen's tale is a case in point.[2]

By the 1950s the Danish writer Karen Blixen (alias Isak Dinesen) was an internationally acclaimed story-teller, chiefly on the basis of two collections of tales, *Seven Gothic Tales* from 1934 (Danish version: *Syv fantastiske Fortællinger*, 1935) and *Winter's Tales* (*VinterEventyr*) from 1942, but her fame rested also on *Out of Africa* (*Den afrikanske Farm*), in which she recounts her experiences as the proprietor of a coffee plantation in Kenya from 1914 to 1931. After her return to Denmark she lived at Rungstedlund, on the eastern seacoast of Sjælland, between Copenhagen and Elsinore. Born in 1885, this is where she died in 1962. By then her health had seriously declined, but she had many international contacts and was visited by many celebrities, and her name was frequently mentioned as a candidate for the Nobel Prize for Literature. A famous photograph from her tour of the United States in 1958 shows her in the company of Marilyn Monroe and Arthur Miller at a lunch party arranged by Carson McCullers.

Among her distinguished friends and visitors was John Gielgud. They had first met in 1939 when he came to Denmark to play Hamlet at Elsinore. When Karen Blixen visited England in 1957, he invited her to Stratford to see a production of *The Tempest* with Gielgud himself playing the part of Prospero. This experience inspired her to write a story which she called 'Tempests' and included in her last collection of tales, *Anecdotes of Destiny* (1958).[3]

Like the better known story from *Anecdotes of Destiny*, 'Babette's Feast', 'Tempests' is set in nineteenth-century Norway. The story opens with an account of a Danish actor-manager, Herr Soerensen, who relinquishes his career in Copenhagen to tour the small towns on the coast of Norway with his own company. When he decides to do *The Tempest* with himself in the leading role, he chooses for the part of Ariel a recent and somewhat unlikely addition to his troupe. Malli is a local girl who has grown up in a small community as the daughter of a Norwegian woman and a Scottish captain who stayed briefly in the little seacoast village, married her, and left her never to return. When Malli is a young girl, she happens to attend a performance by Herr Soerensen's visiting theatrical company; she is immediately stage-struck and hesitantly accepted by the manager.

Malli, a strapping young girl, is not the obvious choice for the airy spirit, but in Herr Soerensen's eyes she is ideal for the role, for as he says, 'it is the words of the poet which are to make Ariel fly' (p. 77; section 2: A Part Assigned),[4] and he struggles to perfect her in the part. Before the opening night, however, the steamer runs into a terrific storm on its way to Christianssand and runs aground, but almost miraculously the ship is saved with all passengers and crew, thanks to the combined efforts of Malli and Ferdinand, a young sailor.

After her heroic deed Malli is carried in the arms of Arndt, the son of Jochum Hosewinckel, the ship's owner, and she is admitted as a favoured guest in his household. At a ball given in her honour she undertakes to entertain with Ariel's song 'Come unto these yellow sands', and Arndt falls in love with her, and soon they are engaged to be married. However, while Arndt is away on a business trip, Malli learns that Ferdinand, the young sailor she assisted during the night of the tempest, has died from injuries he suffered that night, and she is noticeably changed by this knowledge. To lighten her mood the old ship-owner gets into the habit of telling her stories from the old days. One of them is about an eighteenth-century ancestor, Jens Aabel, who once changed the course of the wind and the fire raging in the town by pleading his righteous life in an appeal to the forces of nature. This same Jens Aabel was in the habit of consulting his Bible, in the manner of *sortes sacrae*, when facing important decisions, and the Bible as well as the habit remains in the Hosewinckel family. Not surprisingly Malli cannot resist the temptation to consult the family Bible in this manner. What she finds is, at least for the time being, not revealed, but the following day she seeks out Herr Soerensen and explains to him that now, after Ferdinand's death and in spite of, or indeed because of her love for Arndt, she must go away. That is what she learnt from Jens Aabel: a righteous man may halt a gale,

> 'But I!' she lamented. 'Our gale of Kvasefjord came straight to where I was. Yet I never prayed God to send it, I swear that I never did.'
>
> (p. 138; section 16: Pupil and Master).

At this point her parentage, out of the sea, as it were, becomes significant. Her father, the Scottish captain, who arrived from across the seas and left again the same way never to return, has always been dear to her, though people told stories about him. Now she feels that she too is destined to bring misery and misfortune not only on Ferdinand but also on Arndt: '"I betray them all, as Father betrayed Mother!"' (p. 139). She, too, came as a stranger from across the sea and captivated Arndt, but she is bound to release him again. The following and final section of the story is in the form of a valedictory letter she writes to Arndt, in which she explains that although she loves him dearly she must act upon her 'deception' of him and go away. This had become quite clear to her when she had consulted Jens Aabel's Bible.

This outline of the plot of 'Tempests' does not capture the complexity of this anecdote of destiny and the many layers it works on. From her early youth Blixen had had a deep knowledge and love of Shakespeare, but until the above-mentioned occasion she had not had a chance to see a performance of *The Tempest*.[5] The appropriation of Shakespeare's text for the tale Blixen set about writing soon after is explicit and obvious, but at the same time indirect, subtle, and not easy to fathom.

Blixen's use of Shakespeare's play ignores many aspects which have been foregrounded in recent studies of *The Tempest*, such as the post-colonial interest in the relationship between Prospero and Caliban, but it also leaves out themes crucial to earlier readings which have centred on Caliban's role in the play.[6] It is clearly Ariel's role which inspired Blixen's imagination. It is the fate of her 'Ariel' (Malli) and to a certain extent her relationship with 'Prospero' (Herr Soerensen) which concern Blixen's appropriation of Shakespeare.

However, in the texture of Blixen's anecdote of destiny Shakespeare's Ariel is woven together with other highly suggestive narrative strands. Her Ariel is less the airy spirit than a being associated with the sea. It is worth noting, though, that Shakespeare's Ariel, the spirit of transformation, appears in the shape of a nymph of the sea prior to his enticement of Ferdinand, even if he is invisible to Ferdinand when he sings to him. Arriving in Christianssand after her heroic behaviour at sea in the storm, Malli is described as an angel 'revealed in the likeness of a young seaman' (p. 94; section 7: For Bravery). She is the daughter of the mysterious Scottish sea-captain, who had won his wife's assent by linking the beat of the waves to the beat of the heart, and she is, not least to Arndt, a creature 'slung into his embrace by the sea itself' (p. 95). Her destiny is strangely anticipated by that of Arndt's first love Guro, who drowns herself, feeling that 'I am a lost creature, because I have met you and have looked at you, Arndt!' (p. 102). Like her father, Malli leaves as she arrived, across the water.

Her fate is also anticipated in the description of her early in the story as a young lioness:

> And as now here Malli's story is being written and read, one is free to imagine that had it drawn out longer she would have become what the French call *une lionne*, a lioness. In the story itself she is but a lion-cub, somewhat whelp-like in movement and, up to the last chapter, uncertain in her estimation of her own strength.
>
> (p. 83; section 3: The Child of Love).

In the last section it is revealed that when she opened the Bible at random the scriptural passage she struck upon was the opening verses of the Book of Isaiah, chapter 29, which (Blixen cites the Authorized Version) run as follows

> Woe to Ariel, to Ariel!... And thou shalt be brought down, and thou shalt speak out of the ground ... and thy voice shall be as of one that hath a familiar spirit, out of the ground, and thy speech shall whisper out of the dust!
>
> (pp. 147-48; section 17: The Last Letter)

In the Bible Ariel, a name for Jerusalem, means 'God's lion'. Malli the lion-cub identifies with the biblical Ariel, explaining to Herr Soerensen her need to depart as she will otherwise bring misfortune and misery on Arndt: 'For I speak as one that has a familiar spirit, out of the ground' (p. 139; Section 16: Pupil and Master).

The biblical implications of the name Ariel enrich the story, but only as a complement to the Shakespearean signification. The use of Shakespeare's *The Tempest*, which is implied in the title, is quite explicit on the plot level when Herr Soerensen decides to realize his dream, and Malli is chosen to play the part of Ariel. The successful endeavour to ensure that everybody on board is brought safely ashore is the first obvious indication that Malli has embarked on a kind of identification with the character of Ariel.

When at the ball given in her honour she sings Ariel's song 'Come unto these yellow sands', Arndt falls in love with her. Arndt is consistently presented as a young prince, and for a brief while it seems that Malli is destined to play the part of Miranda to his Ferdinand, and that Herr Soerensen is to become her Prospero-like father figure and give her up to the young man. When the two young lovers call upon him, he takes leave of her using lines from *The Tempest*: 'Why, that's my dainty Ariel! I shall miss thee!' (5.1.95). Subsequently he dreams of her situation and his own part in it in terms based on the play, and he ponders on the links between play world and real world:

> The whole world, the everyday common life, lifted onto the stage and being made one with it. Thy will be done, Willliam Shakespeare, as on the stage so also in the drawing-room! Here in very reality his Ariel did spread out a pair of wings and did rise into the air straight before his eyes.
>
> (p. 107; section 10: Exchange of Visits)

This notion does not, however, stay with him for long: 'For it was more likely that daily life would drag down the stage to its own level than that the stage would succeed in maintaining it so highly elevated'. Fearing that he will lose his Ariel and that his great enterprise will founder, he wonders why reality, the tempest in Kvasefjord, must 'break right into the middle of his William's *Tempest*? Could it be that it had been brought about by the will of that forceful, fearless, formidable child?' (p. 108).

However, Malli's escape into the role of young lover, a Miranda or even a Juliet, does not last very long. The death of Ferdinand changes that. She knows this is so, she tells Herr Soerensen; for, as she explains to him '"I speak as one that has a familiar spirit, out of the ground"' (p. 139: section 16: Pupil and Master). The meaning of these strange words is made clear later (p. 147) when in her farewell letter to Arndt she quotes at greater length the scriptural passage she hit upon: 'Woe to Ariel, to Ariel! ...' These and other verses from the prophet's mouth make Malli realize that no common future is possible for Arndt and her. She can never give him satisfaction. In her letter to him, she cites from Isaiah 29:8, and comments:

> 'It shall even be as when an hungry man dreameth, and behold, he eateth; but he awaketh, and his soul is empty; or as when as a thirsty man dreameth, and behold, he drinketh; but he awaketh, and behold, he is faint, and his soul hath appetite.'

Yes, Arndt, this is as it would come to be with you if you kept me, and no otherwise.

(p. 148; section 17: The Last Letter)

She is like a dream vision or a fiction that he cannot hold on to, and in a few lines of simple verse she tells him that they must part:

> I have made you poor, my sweetheart dear.
> I am far from you when I am near.
> I have made you rich, my dearest heart.
> I am near when we are far apart. (p. 149)

What above all puzzles and disturbs her is the fact that in the storm she did not really act heroically, because she was not in the least afraid, and this absence of fear made her an outcast among ordinary people. The reason for that was that in the storm she experienced it all as Ariel, who when the ship went down 'could fly off and wing my way from her' (p. 149). Later, as a kind of postscript she concludes her loving farewell letter to Arndt with the thought that in another such storm she will understand that it is not a play in the theatre, but it is death. 'And it seems to me that then, in the last moment before we go down, I can in all truth be yours. And I am thinking that it will be fine and great to let wave-beat cover heart-beat' (p. 151). But right now she must go away, 'for I belong elsewhere and must now go there' (p. 150).

Clearly, her identification with Ariel has become her destiny. It is the dream and the destiny of the airy spirit to yearn for release. Prospero and Ariel are alike artists, and as such they must miss, shun, and escape from ordinary human contacts: 'If I do not go away I shall bring misfortune upon him. Oh, misfortune and misery, Herr Soerensen!' (p.139). Herr Soerensen, who left not only Denmark, but a loving wife, understands this. In the crucial penultimate section of the story, called 'Pupil and Master', the direct allusions to and quotations from Shakespeare's play are very frequent and explicit. In the intimate atmosphere between him and the girl he sees their situation and their relationship in terms of Prospero and Ariel:

> And with Prospero's mantle round his shoulders, without lessening his pity of the despairing girl by his side, he was aware of a growing, happy consciousness of fulfillment and reunion. He was not to abandon his precious possession, but she was still his and would remain with him, and he was to see his life's great project realised.
>
> (p. 141; section 16: Pupil and Master).

He outlines his plans for her escape, asking her, in Prospero's words (to Miranda; 1, 2, 170) to 'sit still, and hear the last of our sea-sorrow'. In the mosaic of lines from Ariel's part which Malli goes on to quote back at him she stresses the spirit's worthy service, and she ends by changing Ariel's song addressed to Ferdinand into a comment on her own transformation into the spirit of artistic creation:

'Full fathom five my body lies,
Of my bones are coral made,
Those are pearls that were my eyes,
Nothing of me that doth fade,
But doth suffer a sea-change
Into something rich and strange.
Sea-nymphs hourly ring my knell.
Hark! now I hear them – ding dong bell!'

Herr Soerensen's role, playing the part of Prospero and speaking his lines to Ariel, is to set her free, so that they together can escape from Christianssand and pursue their artistic dreams. She asks him why it must be like that and he, who has formed the habit of speaking in blank verse at heightened moments of being, answers her:

"O girl, be silent. We must never question – it is the others shall come questioning us – it is our noble privilege to answer – o answers fine and clear, o wondrous answers! – the questions of a baffled and divided – humanity. And ne'er ourselves to ask " (p. 145).

And when she asks him what they are to get in return, he concludes: 'And in return we get the world's distrust – and our dire loneliness. And nothing else' (p. 146).

Karen Blixen's appropriation of Shakespeare's play builds on and develops the familiar idea of Prospero the Magus as a representative of the Artist: the playwright, the director, the actor. In her anecdote of destiny, however, the emphasis has shifted from Prospero to Ariel, or more precisely to the girl chosen to play the part of Ariel.

Shakespeare's Ariel is perhaps primarily created to be an instrument of carrying out Prospero's intentions, demonstrating his magical powers. The character has, however, been given traces of individual life. The airy spirit is epicene, and though the part was written to be performed by a male actor, Ariel has frequently been played by a girl or woman. In the master-servant relationship Ariel is affectionate and obedient, but also slightly recalcitrant. There has been a tendency to pair and contrast Ariel with Prospero's other servant, Caliban, as emblematic of the elements, and there have also been attempts, on the stage and in the study, to see them as complementary figures functioning less as individuals than as representations of aspects of Prospero himself.[7] In quite different ways they share a yearning for freedom from bondage, and Ariel has been seen and appropriated as an emblem of the pursuit of (political) freedom.⁸ In Blixen's version of the story, where Caliban plays no role at all, Ariel and the identification with Ariel have different implications. It is not Ariel's yearning for freedom that is in focus, but the need, or indeed the destiny, of the person who plays and becomes Ariel to set herself free of ties to other human beings, irrespective of the cost.

Malli's keenness and Malli's imagination are so strong that in a real-life storm at sea and shipwreck her performance is governed by her imagined identification with Ariel. Throughout the story the forces of destiny and providence are brought into play, but especially important is the idea that it is her destiny to be Ariel. Though the real-life sequence of events seems to cast her in a Miranda-like role, the pull of destiny is too strong: she is fated to be Ariel, the free and independent spirit, on stage and in life, with all the joy and freedom, all the suffering, and all the seclusion of an aery spirit denied intimate human relationships. For as she explains to Arndt in her letter, she has come to see that

> in a human being it is beautiful to fear, and also I see clearly that the one who does not fear is all alone, and is rejected, an outcast from among people. But I, I was not in the least afraid.
>
> (p. 149; section 17: The Last Letter)

As usual, Karen Blixen has left an open field for interpretations, and not surprisingly the story has been subjected to a great number of interpretations by a variety of scholars and critics, who all address themselves more or less directly to the question of Blixen's use of Shakespeare's play.

In her admirable biography of Karen Blixen, *Isak Dinesen: The Life of Karen Blixen* (1982) Judith Thurman devotes an entire chapter to a discussion and interpretation of this story.⁹ Thurman's approach is, in accordance with the context for which it was written, chiefly biographical. The story of Malli is seen as a rendering of Blixen's views on her own life and the stages in her development into an artist. It is, however, also made clear that the story grew out of Gielgud's invitation to her to see the performance of *The Tempest* at Stratford in 1957. It is very probable that Karen Blixen, as Judith Thurman claims in her reading of the story, was attracted to the material and shaped it the way she did because she saw in Malli's fate a reflection of her own condition, especially her questionable relationship to a 'demonic' father, but also the idea that love between human beings must be sacrificed for the sake of art.

The dichotomy between life and art is undoubtedly at the heart of the tale. Most critics see this as the central idea in the story, though with varying interpretations. Robert Langbaum stresses that Malli must learn not to confuse life and art.[10] In the storm, playing Ariel, she did that, but the storm that fulfilled her deepest wish killed Ferdinand. At the end she leaves Arndt because she has realized the difference between life and art. If she stays, he will be like the biblical dreamer who wakes up hungry.

Toril Moi's reading is based on Freudian psychoanalysis. It sees Malli as 'art's martyr', who gives up the happiness of love to submit to her destiny.[11] Illusion, or fiction, is at the same time inadequate to and transcending the demands of ordinary life. The true artist must live in the agony of this split.

In Grethe Rostbøll's view Malli realizes that love will tie her down to a bourgeois life and feels instinctively the need to break loose and follow her destiny.[12]

Hans Holmberg sees the story in a thematic context rooted in 'a personal, existential conflict concerning the liberating power of art'.[13] Whereas other Blixen stories confirm this power, 'Tempests' rejects it. His argument hinges on the contrast between the Shakespearean and the Biblical implications of the figure of Ariel. Holmberg points out that the famous nineteenth-century Danish actress, Johanne Louise Heiberg, had used the same Biblical quotation from Isaiah to argue the need to anchor artistic endeavour in a moral commitment to reality. He demonstrates Blixen's familiarity with Heiberg's text and argues her indebtedness to Heiberg in 'Tempests': Malli's reductive view of art is also Karen Blixen's towards the end of her life. The conflict is certainly crucial to the story, but it seems to me that Holmberg ignores the sense of destiny in Malli's decision, whatever the limitations of her choice of art over life.

Contrary to these four interpretations Tone Selboe takes the end of the story to signify that it is not for the sake of art that Malli parts with love and life, but that she returns to her father, the representative of the sea, disappearance and death.[14]

In her letter to Arndt, Malli says 'you cannot keep me, for I belong elsewhere and must now go there' (p. 150). The meaning of 'belonging elsewhere' is crucial to the understanding of the story's outcome. It is quite possible to see this as her yearning to join her elusive father, who is not only her Shakespearean hero (cf p. 82), but also a mythical Flying Dutchman, a man of the sea. In the context, however, a more probable explanation of her sense of belonging elsewhere is with her fictional father, in the world of art, 'the lovely island full of tones, sounds and music sweet', the setting of Shakespeare's *Tempest*, which Malli refers to immediately before these lines. But then, in the last paragraphs of the story Malli suggests that some day she may be emancipated from the role of Ariel and wake up to reality.

Running into another storm she may clearly understand that it is not a play in the theatre, but it is death:

> And it seems to me that then, in the last moment before we go down, I can in all truth be yours. And I am thinking that it will be fine and great to let wave-beat cover heart-beat. And in that hour to say: 'I have been saved, because I have met you and have looked at you, Arndt!' (p. 151)

The encounter with Shakespeare's play provided Blixen with an opportunity to embody her ideas and experiences with appropriate artistic distance in a story at once specific and universal. Her use of Shakespeare's story is highly selective; there is nothing about Caliban, and nothing about retribution in it. It is also highly suggestive. Shakespeare's Ariel combined with the biblical Ariel gave her the material to describe a young woman who faced the consequences of identifying herself as an elusive and creative airy spirit. The appropriation of *The Tempest* added to her story the resonances and the universality which pervade this anecdote of destiny about the tensions in the interplay of life and art.

Notes

[1] Virginia Mason Vaughan and Alden T. Vaughan eds., *The Tempest* (Walton-on-Thames: Thomas Nelson and Sons, 1999).
[2] Inga-Stina Ewbank discusses the debt to *The Tempest* in three Scandinavian texts - Strindberg's *A Dream Play*, Ibsen's *When We Dead Awaken* and Blixen's 'Tempests' - in 'The Tempest and After' in Stanley Wells, ed., *Shakespeare Survey 43*, (Cambridge: Cambridge University Press, 1991).
[3] Unlike most of Blixen's stories 'Tempests' was first written in Danish and called 'Storme'. The collection was first published in Danish as *Skæbne-Anekdoter* in 1958.
[4] All references are to Isak Dinesen, *Anecdotes of Destiny*, (Harmondsworth: Penguin, 1986). For easy reference to other editions I add the relevant number and title of the section in question.
[5] Karen Blixen's lifelong interest in Shakespeare is dealt with sporadically by Judith Thurman in *Isak Dinesen: The Life of Karen Blixen* first published in 1982 (Harmondsworth: Penguin, 1984). Published in Danish with the title *Karen Blixen, en fortællers liv* (Copenhagen: Gyldendal, 1983). Parmenia Migel also deals with this in her *Titania: The biography of Isak Dinesen* (New York: Random House, 1967). Migel (in an unidentified quotation, p. 16) writes that for Blixen the discovery of Shakespeare at the age of fourteen 'was one of the really great events in my life.' Bernhard Glienke has a complete list of Blixen's references to Shakespeare in *Fatale Präzedenz, Karen Blixens Mythologie*, Band 18 in *Skandinavistische Studien* (Neumünster: Karl Wachholtz Verlag, 1986), v. esp. pp. 171-77. Glienke quotes

from a letter Karen Blixen wrote to her sister in 1930, in which she associates the airborne Denys Finch Hatton with Ariel.

[6] E.g. in Frank Kermode's Introduction to the Arden edition of *The Tempest* (1954, rev. ed. 1961.)

[7] Cf. the New Cambridge Shakespeare edition of *The Tempest*, ed. by David Lindley (Cambridge: Cambridge University Press, 2002). In the introduction Lindley discusses Caliban and Ariel. In The New Arden Shakespeare (Introduction, pp. 27-29) the editors comment on Ariel's name with reference to the biblical context.

[8] E. g. by the Uruguayan writer José Enrique Rodó in his *Ariel* (1900): 'Shakespeare's ethereal Ariel symbolizes the noble, soaring aspect of the human spirit'. Cf Appendix 2 in the Arden 3 edition, pp. 325-31, and the editors' comment, p. 99.

[9] Judith Thurman, *Isak Dinesen*, section 49.

[10] Robert Langbaum, *The Gayety of Vision, A Study of Isak Dinesen's Art* (London: Chatto and Windus, 1964; New York: Random House, 1965). Published in Danish with the title *Mulm, stråler og latter* (Copenhagen: Gyldendal, 1964).

[11] Toril Moi, '"Hele verden en scene": En analyse af Karen Blixens "Storme"', *Edda 86, Hefte 2*, (Oslo, 1986).

[12] Grethe F. Rostbøll, *Længslens Vingeslag: analyser af Karen Blixens fortællinger*, (København: Gyldendal, 1996).

[13] Hans Holmberg, *Ingen skygge uden lys: om livets veje og kunstens i nogle fortællinger af Karen Blixen* (Copenhagen: Reitzels Forlag, 1995).

[14] Tone Selboe, *Kunst og erfaring, en studie i Karen Blixens forfatterskap* (Odense: Odense Universitetsforlag, 1996). Other detailed discussions of the story are Nadia Setti, 'Visions of life's tempest: from Shakespeare to Karen Blixen' in Susan Sellers (ed.), *Writing Differences, Readings from the seminar of Hélène Cixous* (New York: St. Martin's Press, 1988) and Judith Lee, 'Rough Magic: Isak Dinesen's Re-visions of *The Tempest*' in Marianne Novy (ed.), *Cross-Cultural Performances, Differences in Women's Re-visions of Shakespeare* (Urbana and Chicago: University of Illinois Press, 1993).

BOOK REVIEW

Russell Duncan & Clara Juncker editors, *Transnational America: Contours of Modern US Culture*. Copenhagen: Museum Tusculanum Press, 2004. 276 pp.: color photos; ISBN 87 7289 958 1. 198 d.kr.

Globalization is a phenomenon that increasingly preoccupies academia as well as society at large.. The Internet, free trade, increased immigration, and terrorism are among the manifestations of globalization that make it impossible to ignore the rapid changes that are occurring in our world. The United States is usually seen as the prime mover in this process. The editors of *Transnational America* acknowledge this and point out "…that the nation we identify as the United States of America is in the world in ways that others are not." This necessitates focusing on the United States to allow for a fuller understanding of globalization. In doing this, however, the authors of the thirteen essays in this collection remind us that the United States is as much a site being shaped by globalizing forces as it is its agent.

The essays are organized into four sections: Visions and Revisions, Secrets and Lies, New People, and New Places. Also included is a photo-essay consisting of mainly color photos, each accompanied by short explanations that serve as companions to each essay. In "Visions and Revisions," four essays explore some of the broader aspects of American identity. Although each essay is ostensibly concerned with contemporary aspects of globalization and identity formation, they all end up anchoring current circumstances in ongoing historical discourses. Paul Levine, in "Americanization and Globalization," responds to those who use the term "Americanization" in the pejorative sense by discussing the syncretic composition of American mass culture. The American mass culture that arouses the suspicion and hostility of many has itself been, and continues to be, honed by transnational crosscurrents. It is also subject to further erosion and remolding when projected outside of the United States. Obododimma Oha, in "The Future of the Past: Christian Cultural Reproduction of America," also detects historical continuity in Christian efforts to define American identity. Beginning with recent Christian docu-dramatic productions that attempt to reinforce their vision of American colonization and ascendancy, Oha takes us back to Columbus in order to comment on the splicing of Christianity with American identity. Marie Anderson, in "National History/Transnational Themes: Inaugural Addresses and American Mythology," explores the symbolic importance of the presidency in reflecting aspects of American identity. Specifically, she examines how presidents use their inaugural addresses to frame their own identity within the context of American myth. In "Trading People: Slavery and Migration in the 21st Century" Carl Pedersen addresses one of the darkest aspects of globalization. Placing America and globalization in a historical context, he contends that recent neo-liberal policies have resulted in a process of global human exploitation that echoes that of the Atlantic slave trade and the colonial land grab of the late Victorian era.

"Secrets and Lies" consists of three essays that grapple with several bogeymen of the American subconscious. In "Conspiracy Theories in America: Two Approaches," Erik Åsard compares and contrasts competing approaches to the American propensity to indulge in conspiracy theories - a propensity that has only been heightened due to recent globalization – and argues that conspiracy thinking needs to be taken seriously as an area of study. Claudia Egerer turns to the works of Paul Auster and Don DeLillo in "The Image of Terror/Terrorism of Images in *Leviathan* and *Mao II*". She details how the two works – written before 9/11 and yet in ways anticipating it – deal with the interplay between media images and terrorism. Finally, Clara Juncker's "Not a Story to Pass on?: Tim O'Brien's Vietnam," revisits America's unhealed wound, the still unresolved legacy of Vietnam.

The focus of the collection narrows in its second half to specific places and individuals (and groups) in the sections "New People" and "New Places." "Framing Hillary Rodham Clinton" by Raili Põldsaar, "Woman's Place in a New World: Scandinavian-American Visions, 1850-1900" by Jørn Brøndal and "Muhammad Ali, Southerner" by Stuart Kidd are all essays that illuminate the persons in question while also contributing to an understanding of the more general issues embedded in their experiences. Martyn Bone's "The Transnational Turn in the South: Region, Nation, Globalization," Russell Duncan's "Crossing Borders: Hispanic Atlanta, 1900-2004," and Justin D. Edwards' "Nordcities; or, the American City in Canada," all employ place as a means of understanding American culture and transnational forces. There are four essays that are mainly concerned - or at least partly in the case of "Framing Hillary Rodham Clinton" - with the South. Considering that the region has perennially been regarded as the most insulated from transnational forces such as immigration, it is important to recognize that the South has also experienced transnational influences and is increasingly being shaped by them.

Transnational America makes a serious and timely contribution to American Studies. The essays, taken both as a whole and individually, are potentially valuable tools for those working within the field. It is easy to criticize a collection of essays for its omissions, particularly when taking on a topic of such broad and nebulous scope. The essays have been well selected. and provide research that is broadly representative of the many domains of American Studies. The inclusion of essays concerned with the South is a major advantage in the light of the region's rise in national influence and the confluence there of transnational, as well as trans-regional, forces. Many of the essays could be used as instructional material. Offering up-to-date research on a variety of contemporary issues, the volume points readers both to important sources concerning a variety of transnational topics, and to other topics yet to be researched.

David Harding

NOTES ON CONTRIBUTORS

Paul Edmondson, M.A., Ph.D., is Head of Education at the Shakespeare Birthplace Trust, Stratford-upon-Avon. He is co-author (with Stanley Wells) of *Shakespeare's Sonnets* (Oxford, 2004). His book on *Twelfth Night: A Performance Handbook* is due to be published by Palgrave Macmillan in 2005. He is an Honorary Fellow of the Shakespeare Institute, University of Birmingham and Assistant Director of the Stratford-upon-Avon Poetry Festival.

Dorrit Einersen is Senior Lecturer in the Department of English, University of Copenhagen. Her primary interests are medieval literature and women's literature from the 19th and 20th centuries. Her recent publications include 'Jeanette Winterson's *Oranges are not the only Fruit*. The quest for the self' in *Proceedings from the 8th Nordic Conference on English Studies*, edited by Karin Aijmer and Britta Olinder (Göteborg University Press, 2003) and 'Translation as Apology or Cover. Chaucer's *Troilus and Criseyde*' in *Pratiques de Traduction au Moyen Age / Medieval Translation Practices*, ed. Peter Andersen (Museum Tusculanum Press, 2004).

Niels Bugge Hansen retires in 2005 from a position as Associate Professor in English literature at the University of Copenhagen. One of his major fields of interest and research is Shakespearean studies, and in recent years he has written a number of articles on the reception (translation, performance, and appropriation) of Shakespeare in Denmark.

David Harding is Foreign Lecturer in the Department of English, Aarhus University. His main areas of research are within American and Canadian Studies, with a particular focus on Native Americans/First Nations and the environment. He has recently published work on the Navajo, the Cree of Northern Quebec, Leslie Marmon Silko's *Almanac of the Dead* and English colonial discourse in Ireland and North America.

Søs Haugaard is an external lecturer at the University of Copenhagen. She has taught both graduate and undergraduate courses in English literature, including Shakespeare, at the universities of Copenhagen and Reading, and at the University of Southern Denmark where she is currently working for her Ph. D. Søs Haugaard is the chairman of the Danish Shakespeare Society.

Peter Holland is McMeel Family Professor in Shakespeare Studies in the Department of Film, Television, and Theatre of the University of Notre Dame. He was Director of the University of Birmingham's Shakespeare Institute in Stratford-upon-Avon from 1997 to 2002. He is editor of *Shakespeare Survey* and general editor of *Redefining British Theatre History* for Palgrave MacMillan and (with Stanley Wells) of Oxford Shakespeare Topics for Oxford University Press. His current project is editing *Coriolanus* for the Arden Shakespeare 3rd series.

Lars Kaaber is a Danish writer, playwright, and a theatre director with sixty-five productions to his credit. His stagings of Shakespeare include *Measure for Measure* in 1994 and again in 2002, *A Midsummer Night's Dream* in 1996, *The Winter's Tale* (1998), *Twelfth Night* (1999) and *As You Like It* (2000). He also directed an international production of Rossini's opera *Otello* in 2000, and was Shakespeare consultant on Dogme film IV, *The King is Alive* (2000). His books on Shakespearean drama have been published by Hernovs Forlag.

Charles Lock is Professor of English Literature at the University of Copenhagen. Recent publications include a number of essays on Nigerian literature, an article on the medieval mystical treatise, *The Cloud of Unknowing*, and a foreword to a volume of poems by Anne Blonstein, *worked on screen* (Poetry Salzburg 2005).

Viggo Hjørnager Pedersen is an Associate Professor in English at the University of Copenhagen. He was awarded a Ph. D. in translation studies in 1991, and obtained his second doctorate (Dr. Phil.) from the University of Southern Denmark in 2004 for a monograph on the English translations of Hans Christian Andersen's tales and stories. He has twice edited the Vinterberg and Bodelsen Danish-English dictionary, in 1990 and 1998.He has written widely on English literature and translation studies. He is also a professional translator, and has translated a number of English novels into Danish. He is currently engaged in research into English translations of Hans Christian Andersen.

Tom Pettitt is an Associate Professor at the Institute for Literature, Media and Cultural Studies of the University of Southern Denmark, where he contributes courses on late-medieval and early-modern literature and theatre to the English programmes in Odense and Kolding. He is also associated with the Centre for Medieval Studies at SDU's Odense campus. His research focuses on folk traditions of narrative (e.g. wondertales and urban legends), song (particularly ballads) and dramatic customs (e.g. charivaries and mummers' plays), both as cultural products in their own right, and in relation to conventional literary and theatre history.

Michael Skovmand is Associate Professor in the Department of English, University of Aarhus. He has edited various publications (*The Angry Young Men, George Orwell and 1984, Media Fictions, Media Cultures, Screen Shakespeare*), and has contributed to such periodicals as *Essays and Studies, Nordicom Review, Shakespeare Yearbook* and *Nordic Journal of English Studies*.

Robert Weimann is Professor Emeritus of the University of California, Irvine, and the *Forschungsschwerpunkt Literaturwissenschaft*, Berlin. He is currently engaged in a project entitled "Shakespeare and the Power of Performance." His recent publications include *Author's Pen and Actor's Voice. Playing and Writing in Shakespeare's Theatre* (2000) and *Prologues to Shakespeare's Theatre. Performance and Liminality in Early Modern Drama*, together with Douglas Bruster (2004). He was awarded an honorary doctorate and is an honorary member of the Modern Language Association of America (since 1985) and (since 1992) a member of the Berlin-Brandenburg Academy of Fine Arts.

FORTHCOMING ISSUES

- *Studies in Translation*
  Volume 6, 2006
  Editor: Ida Klitgård

- *The State of the Union: 1707-2007*:
  Volume 7, 2007
  Editors: Jørgen Sevaldsen and Jens Rahbek Rasmussen